The
Racing Rules
for Sailors

The
Racing Rules
for Sailors

**A complete guide
1997–2000**

Mary Pera

ADLARD COLES NAUTICAL
London

Published 1997 by Adlard Coles Nautical
an imprint of A & C Black (Publishers) Ltd
35 Bedford Row, London WC1R 4JH

Copyright © Mary Pera 1997
Rules extracts copyright © ISAF 1997

First edition published by Nautical Books 1985
Second edition 1989
Third edition published by Adlard Coles Nautical 1993

ISBN 0–7136–4608 X

A CIP catalogue record for this book is available from the British Library.
Typeset in 10½ on 11¼ Sabon by Florencetype Ltd, Stoodleigh, Devon
Printed and bound in Great Britain by Page Bros, Norwich

Contents

Acknowledgements

The fourth edition of this book brings it into line with the changes finalized by the ISAF in November 1996 and, as far as possible, with those occasioned by the new editions of the RYA and US Sailing appeal cases, at present being revised; thus it keeps pace with the expansion of sailing and the development of the sport represented by the fundamental rewriting of the rules that has taken place.

I am very much aware that a large part of the book is not written by me. The many extracts from the appeal cases were written over the last 30 years in a number of countries by devoted, unpaid, and often anonymous judges. They have unstintingly given their time on appeals committees and protest committees to try to ensure fair results in competitions that range from the humblest club racing to the Olympic Games. Many of these judges are friends and colleagues, and I am most grateful to them for expressing points much better than I could do myself. I am also grateful to the various national authorities and the ISAF for permission to publish extracts from the cases. My thanks are also due to John Doerr for checking the draft of Part 2.

Mary Pera
February 1997

Preface

For most of the last century, when boat racing as we know it began, each club drafted its own rules, usually adapting the rule of the road at sea to the requirements of racing. It was only in 1875, after a number of false starts, that 'The Yacht Racing Association' was formed in Britain to codify the rules and alter them when necessary. Within seven years, every British club had adopted the rules of the YRA (now RYA).

In 1907, similar developments elsewhere saw the beginning of international co-operation, mainly in Europe, with the formation of the IYRU (now ISAF) which writes and publishes the rules we use today. However, it was not until 1950 that the IYRU and the North American Yacht Racing Union (later to separate into the CYA and the USYRU, now US Sailing) began to combine their rules, and only in 1959 did the rules become universal. Today all water-borne sailing boats – keel boats, dinghies, multihulls, round-the-worlders, even sailboards and radio-controlled model boats – use them; only canoes are separate.

The rules are revised every fourth year after the Olympic Games, and 1997 sees the biggest shake-up in the rules since 1959. Thirty-five years of rules with all their alterations and additions have been torn down and rebuilt from their foundations: the order has been changed from a basically chronological one to an attempt to put first the rules of most importance to the competitor; the language has been simplified – generally speaking, changing from Latin- and French-based words to Anglo-Saxon; and last, and most important, the game on the water has been simplified by a total rewrite of the rules when boats meet. In four years' time we shall see how good a job the rule writers have done.

The ISAF publishes interpretations – that is, case law culled from the appeal cases of the various national authorities. New cases are published each year, and all cases are updated to the latest rules every four years.

Another ISAF publication is the *Umpires' Call Book*; this gives detailed guidance for the many problems that arise exclusively in umpired events.

This book includes the *Racing Rules of Sailing*, including Appendix A, but not the other more specialized appendices. In the commentary

I try to illuminate each rule by throwing new light on it, possibly from a different angle, which may help the reader to understand why the rule is there and what it does. Where possible, the relevant case law is cited. At the time of writing, the national authorities and ISAF have not yet completed the revisions of case law necessary after the rule changes, and I can only hope that all the cases cited in this edition survive to the new editions. The main sources for case law are the ISAF interpretations, and the publications of the RYA, US Sailing and the CYA. The cases are respectively referred to as, for example, ISAF 51, US 123, CYA 44, and RYA 93/6, and so on. My own opinions, identifiable by some phrase as 'I believe' or 'I suppose', are also occasionally expressed. In 1997 the ISAF cases are being renumbered, starting at 1. It is impossible to change them in time for the publication of this book but, since the order is not being changed and the old numbers will still be printed clearly, either series of numbers can be used for the next four years.

It is nowhere written that a protest committee must follow a published decision, but it would be very unwise of it not to do so. ISAF Regulation 12.3.3 merely states: '[the ISAF interpretations of the *Racing Rules of Sailing*] shall be recognised as authoritative interpretations and explanations of the rules'. A national authority appeals committee will be unlikely to upset one of its own rulings, and doubly unlikely to upset one that has been confirmed by the ISAF. Some of these interpretations arise from very unusual one-off incidents; others interpret a common word or phrase, and these, sooner or later, become the basis of a rule change, incorporating the point in question.

Gerald Sambrooke-Sturgess, speaking of the rules in his *Yacht Racing*, says: 'I feel sure no yachtsman would ever be able to remember them all, especially in the excitement of a yacht race . . . I have known a man try to learn the IYRU rules by heart, like a parrot. That is, of course, ridiculous. Some men are always quoting protest cases. That is worse still. They snap at minor points as a dog snaps at flies on a summer's day. That is not the way to understand the rule of the road.' It is still true today, and you can go out and race successfully, up to a certain standard, with only a knowledge of the most basic principles of the rules – thousands do so. However, such competitors may lose places by giving room where there is no need to, and where a more rule-conscious helmsman might well gain a place.

Ignorance of the rules is no excuse, and the more aware a helmsman is of the rules while sailing, the less likely he is to meet disaster in the protest room. The very top helmsmen are so practised that they sail with every detail of the rules clear in their heads to gain, legitimately, every advantage that the wording of the rules permits them.

An incident on the water is often followed, if not by a protest, by a long argument in the bar, and this book should help helmsmen resolve their differences and will also help protest committees to reach good decisions in the shortest possible time. However, it must be remembered that there is no substitute for reading the rules themselves, particularly as many are self-explanatory.

A boat called *Daisy* plays a large part throughout the text of the book; so many sentences would otherwise start 'When a boat . . .' that I have preferred to put 'When *Daisy* . . .' Throughout, boats are feminine, people masculine; this is not meant to be sexist – simply to avoid clumsy references to he/she. It is also following the style used in the *Racing Rules of Sailing* published by the ISAF. The terms 'give-way', 'keep-clear' and 'obligated' are all used to describe the boat that has not got right of way.

I hope this book will help helmsmen, crews, race officers and protest committees to gain further understanding of the rules they are all using so as to increase their enjoyment of racing and its administration.

Standard Abbreviations

Organization
CYA   Canadian Yachting Association
FIV   Federazione Italiana Vela
ISAF   International Sailing Federation
KNVW   Koninklijk Nederlands Watersport Verbond
RYA   Royal Yachting Association
US SAILING   United States Sailing Association

Rules
IRPCS   International Regulations for Preventing Collisions at Sea
RRS   Racing Rules of Sailing

Boats
I   inside
O   outside
P   port tack
S   starboard tack
L   leeward
W   windward
M   middle (or intervening)

The Racing Rules of Sailing
for 1997–2000

Sportsmanship and the Rules

Competitors in the sport of sailing are governed by a body of rules that they are expected to follow and enforce. A fundamental principle of sportsmanship is that when competitors break a rule they will promptly take a penalty or retire.

When a football referee fails to see a foul, the player need not penalize himself, even when he is aware of it; nor need he in many other games. In sailing, though, as also in golf, where much of the game is played out of sight of others, or in a congested area where no referee can get near, the competitor is honour bound to keep the rules. After knowingly breaking a rule in sailing, the competitor should retire or do his turns (or any other penalty imposed by the sailing instructions).

Naturally, the competitor must be sure that he *has* broken a rule. In numerous Part 2 incidents between boats, both helmsmen believe they have right on their side, and then they are fully justified in not taking a penalty but in going to protest to decide the matter. In ISAF 134, a Laser obtained redress and was reinstated when no sound signal accompanied her recall signal and she was unaware that she was over. The RYA's decision stated: 'There is no obligation on a boat to respond when a sound signal is not made, unless she realizes she has started early, when she is bound to retire, or return and start correctly.' Quite recently a young man told me how he had been over the line, but very cleverly had succeeded in hiding behind another boat so that the race officer failed to pick up his sail number. 'But that's cheating,' I exclaimed. First, he looked shocked, then – as I persisted – sheepish, and I hope he will not do it again. It may be clever, but it *is* cheating.

Equally, when a boat hits a mark, or an experienced helmsman infringes rule 43 by pumping, and no penalty is taken, that is cheating, and the competitor is laying himself open to being protested under rule 2 and to the rigours of rule 69. This is illustrated by one interesting case that never came to appeal, so has no formal seal of approval. A boat hit a mark; her helmsman knew it, and was aware of his obligation to retire promptly (no exoneration was permitted), but he did not retire and finished third, getting a gun. He did not tell the race officer afloat or the race committee ashore that he had hit the mark. Finally, when another boat protested him, he retired. The jury decided that the action was a gross breach of good sportsmanship and excluded him from the rest of the regatta under rule 69.

Declarations, often required after long races, should be used to inform the race committee of any infringements such as battery failure – and therefore no lights at night – due to bad weather etc. The race committee will most probably have power to waive or alter penalties in such minor cases.

A young would-be Olympic sailor once asked me whether, if he gave one illegal pump by mistake, he should at once retire. I hardly knew how to answer and thought of the coach's face if such had occurred in a championship. Such a minor slip would, I believe, be forgiven by anyone. Standards of honesty vary, and what one competitor practises (or a coach teaches) may be different from country to country and perhaps from class to class. One thing is certain, though – that as time passes, the cheat and the honest sailor will each come to be recognized for what they truly are and treated accordingly.

Introduction

The Racing Rules of Sailing includes two main sections. The first, Parts 1–7, contains rules that affect all competitors. The second section contains appendices that provide details of rules, rules that apply to particular kinds of racing, and rules that affect only a small number of competitors or officials.

The racing rules are revised and published every four years by the International Sailing Federation (ISAF), the international authority for the sport. This edition becomes effective on 1 April 1997. No changes are contemplated before 2001, but changes determined by the ISAF to be urgent will be made as needed and announced through national authorities.

Terminology   A term used in the sense stated in the Definitions is printed in italics or, in preambles, in bold italics (for example, *racing* and ***racing***). Other words and terms are used in the sense ordinarily understood in nautical or general use. 'Race committee' includes any person or committee performing a race committee function. 'Class rules' includes rules of handicapping and rating systems.

Appendices   When the rules of an appendix apply, they take precedence over any conflicting rules in Parts 1–7. A reference to a rule of an appendix will contain the letter of the appendix and the rule number; for example, 'rule A1.1'. (There is no Appendix I or Appendix O.)

Changes to the Rules   The prescriptions of a national authority, class rules or the sailing instructions may change a racing rule only as permitted in rule 86.

The Introduction to the 1997–2000 racing rules needs no explanation, but it does form part of the rules (see definition Rule) and should be read with care. Note that the term 'race committee' covers all those people who work for the race office, and is discussed under rule 88.1.

Part 1 – Fundamental Rules

1 Safety

Note: it is advisable to read the Definitions on page 143 to clarify terms used. In the ISAF rules a term explained in the Definitions is shown in italic type, or, in the preambles, in bold italic type.

1.1	**Helping Those in Danger** A boat or competitor shall give all possible help to any person or vessel in danger.
1.2	**Life-saving Equipment and Personal Buoyancy** A boat shall carry adequate life-saving equipment for all persons on board, including one item ready for immediate use, unless her class rules make some other provision. Each competitor is individually responsible for wearing personal buoyancy adequate for the conditions.

1.1 Helping Those in Danger

You must always try to rescue a drowning man. By providing both a 'stick' and a 'carrot', the rules do their part to ensure that a fanatic racing skipper does not overlook this. The small 'carrot' can be found in rule 62, where redress is made available to those who help others; this rule is the 'stick'. Disqualifications for failing to help are few and far between, but not unknown. CYA 65 underlines that the help must be unstinting. *Pearce Arrow* broke her mast 500 feet from a lee shore in rough seas and strong winds and asked for help. *Prospector* and *Mustard Seed* did not see the dismasting, but saw the dismasted boat shortly afterwards. *Mustard Seed* was thinking about going to help when a white boat was noticed going to *Pearce Arrow*'s aid. Water in her engine and no suitable chart influenced *Mustard Seed*'s decision not to go. *Prospector* notified the Coast Guard by radio and positioned a crewman on the leeward side to watch, until she also saw the white boat. *Pearce Arrow* later fetched up on the lee shore.

On appeal, the disqualification of *Prospector* and *Mustard Seed* was upheld: 'The issue was whether, on the undisputed facts, the protestees had given "all possible help". In addition to what they did do, they could have closed with *Pearce Arrow* and investigated her need for assistance. By not doing so they failed to ascertain whether more assistance was possible and thereby failed to render "all possible help" . . . their failure to do so was not excused by the fact that the white boat went to the aid of *Pearce Arrow* . . . The protestees had to make a decision in a difficult situation . . . however, the possible grave consequences of one boat failing to investigate the distress call of another compels the Appeals Committee to exact a very high standard of compliance with rule 1.'

(Of course, this case is fine in principle, and no doubt the detailed facts uphold it, but practical people might wonder whether it was not better that *Mustard Seed*, with a dodgy engine and no adequate chart, kept out of trouble.)

In ISAF 38 (discussed later under rule 62), one boat went to help another without being asked. She was considered to be entitled to redress because a boat in a position to help another that may be in danger is bound to do so. 'That she offers assistance not requested is irrelevant.'

CYA 72 further illustrated the rule: one Soling sank another at the finishing line and sailed straight into harbour without stopping to offer help. She was disqualified, notwithstanding the presence of the committee boat.

Rule 62.1(c) makes it clear that a boat is not entitled to redress when she has helped herself or her own crew. This is a logical conclusion when you think about the possible misuse of allowing such an interpretation of the rule. However, while you may not be able to get redress in this situation, what would normally be rule infringements, such as using your engine, are permitted – see rules 41 and 42.3(c).

1.2 Life-saving Equipment and Personal Buoyancy

Life-saving equipment will vary from boat to boat, but it will probably mean at least a lifejacket for each person and a lifebuoy to throw to someone in the water. At a ship's chandlers there is a vast choice. Many sailing instructions and class rules prescribe special safety regulations that detail the requirements for an event or a class. Control was lax in the past, but nowadays, with the increasing likelihood of being sued, race committees check more and more often – so don't be caught out. You are responsible for your own safety in using this equipment. As you fall overboard and float away from your boat, your expensive jacket still on board, you have only yourself to blame. Rule 40 deals with the situation when a race committee orders personal buoyancy to be worn.

2 Fair Sailing

> A boat and her owner shall compete in compliance with recognized principles of sportsmanship and fair play. A boat may be penalized under this rule only if it is clearly established that these principles have been violated.

[Note that the words 'and only when no other rule applies' have gone. This may open the flood gates: a small committee may consider unfair something that is accepted at every big regatta, and there may be some inconsistencies. But the rule has been virtually useless for the last 12 years at least, and it should either come back into use or be deleted.

The words 'except in team racing, by individual effort' have gone. This is not in order to allow one mate to help another, but because this belongs under outside help, rule 41. The team racing appendix (rule D1.1) specifically allows help from a team-mate.]

Let us look at the rule in detail: 'A boat and her owner . . .' The rule is addressed not only, as is usual, to boats (which, as we have seen in the Introduction, includes their crew), but also to the owner because he may not be on board. While boats may not protest under rule 69, they can use rule 2. Thus when John Doe, a crew member of *Buttercup*, is found sawing through *Daisy*'s shrouds during the night, he can be protested directly under this rule. (Of course, if proved, this protest would develop into a '69' for gross misconduct and probably bring John a lengthy ban from ISAF.)

'. . . with recognized principles of sportsmanship and fair play.' No dirty tricks here! In ISAF 107, the experienced helmsman of a port-tack boat hails 'Starboard' to a beginner. The latter, although on starboard tack himself, is bullied into tacking to avoid, as he thinks, a collision. Does the hailing boat infringe the fair sailing rule? The RYA thought so: 'A boat that deliberately hails "Starboard" when she is on port tack has not acted fairly and is liable to disqualification under rule 2.' ISAF 149 and 150 look at two incidents that seem to be superficially alike. In ISAF 149, the crew of L, on a trapeze, deliberately leaned out and touched W's deck with his hand. On appeal, this action was held to have infringed rule 2. On the other hand, in ISAF 150, L, with luffing rights, luffed hard and the helmsman's back touched W just forward of the shroud. Contact could only have been made if L's helmsman was sitting out flat, which was significantly beyond the normal sailing position in the prevailing conditions. L was disqualified and appealed. The appeal was upheld, L was reinstated, and W was penalized under rule 11. 'There is no rule that dictates how a helmsman or crew must sit, and in the absence of any deliberate misuse of the helmsman's positioning, no infringement of rule 2 took place.'

Perhaps the most common query about the use of the rule is when one helmsman sails another off the course and so prevents him, if not from winning, at least from doing his best. It arises most often in the last race of a series when A can win provided B does not win, or is not placed above a certain position, in the last race. A starts correctly and then sits on B, legitimately delaying her opponent provided no rule is broken. Such tactics are accepted (though limited in team and match racing), and delaying an opponent does not of itself infringe rule 2 (RYA 67/13), although it may infringe rule 22. Rule 22 bans interference in two cases: first, between a boat not racing and one that is; and secondly, with a boat that is making her penalty turns.

In RYA 90/6, an incident between two Lasers, S and P, led to a third boat protesting against P for causing S to bear away behind her. P was disqualified under rule 10 and appealed on the grounds that S had chosen not to protest. It was reported, and not denied, that P's representative had been asked by the protest committee if he had broken rule 10 – that is, if he knew that he had broken rule 10 and yet had neither retired nor taken a penalty. His answer was 'yes'. The RYA held that a boat that knows she has broken a rule cannot protect herself from the obligation to take a penalty by citing the absence of a protest from the other boat. P was further disqualified under rule 2.

In RYA 89/13, a boat sailed with her spray hood raised on the downwind leg of a race, but not on the upwind leg. Using standard, designed positions for equipment not restricted by class rules or sailing instructions was held not to infringe rule 2.

Rule A1.3 states that a disqualification under rule 2 cannot be discarded. I believe this might become a harsh provision if a committee were to use the rule indiscriminately.

It must be 'clearly established that these principles have been violated.' Good evidence will be needed before this rule is invoked. When there has been a collision, a rule has nearly always been broken, and someone must be disqualified at the end of the protest even if the jury has had to act on very unsatisfactory evidence. But such unsatisfactory evidence will not be adequate for rule 2, and the more persuasive evidence required for a 'criminal' case is necessary. Furthermore, when the evidence is there, it must then be clear that the facts disclose really unfair sailing and not just close adherence to the rules. Remember always that a disqualification under this rule can easily lead to heavy consequences under rule 69 and is not to be arrived at lightly. In order to improve her own series score, a boat may make it hard for another to do well provided the tactic breaks no other rule (ISAF 155). I wonder if this case would hold good in a handicap event if the hindering boat were bigger and faster than the sat-on boat. Other cases are discussed under rule 69.1.

3 Acceptance of the Rules

> By participating in a race conducted under these racing rules, each competitor and boat owner agrees
>
> (a)   to be governed by the *rules*;
>
> (b)   to accept the penalties imposed and other action taken under the *rules*, subject to the appeal and review procedures provided in them, as the final determination of any matter arising under the *rules*; and
>
> (c)   with respect to such determination, not to resort to any court or other tribunal not provided by the *rules*.

Racing under rules other than those of ISAF must be a rare event, but might lose competitors their ISAF eligibility (Appendix J). When racing under the RRS, each competitor agrees, by the very fact of entering, to follow the rules. He agrees to the protest and appeals systems, and to any penalties he might receive. *Ignorantia juris haud excusat* (ignorance of the law is no excuse) runs the old tag, and the very fact of racing binds him. This mini government by sports authorities is recognized by the legal systems of many countries. If it were not so, sport would be almost impossible. But the sporting bodies, from ISAF itself to the smallest club and its committees, must behave within the rules too.

There are a number of cases now on this subject. The two best known perhaps are the *Satanita* case, which went to the House of Lords 100 years ago and determined in English law that there was an understood contract between boats racing; and the very recent *Charles Jourdain* v *Endeavour* in the USA. This view is now supported by a case in Belgium. In two other cases in the USA, where competitors tried to get decisions by the national authority changed, the courts supported US Sailing. To quote the judgment in *Charles Jourdain* v *Endeavour*: '[Earlier cases] establish the principle that when one voluntarily enters a boat race for which published sailing instructions set out the conditions of participation, a private contract results between the participants requiring their compliance therewith.'

4 Decision to Race

> A boat is solely responsible for deciding whether or not to *start* or to continue *racing*.

The person in charge of a boat must make the decision whether or not to race. In US 209, before the start of the fourth race of a Sunfish series, one boat told the race committee that she thought the weather unsuitable for racing and that the race should not be started. She then withdrew. The race committee ran the race, the Sunfish requested redress in vain, and then appealed. The US Appeals Committee remarked: 'The decision to start, postpone or abandon a race is solely within the jurisdiction of the race committee. If a boat decides not to race, she cannot claim that her finishing position was prejudiced.'

In addition to preventing such claims for redress, the rule protects a race committee in the event of accidents. Only the owner or skipper of a boat can know whether she is seaworthy or not. It would be impossible for a committee to check the soundness of hulls and gear or to judge the competence of crews.

However, if six rescue boats were scheduled to be on the water during an event and only one was there when an accident occurred, the race committee might well have to shoulder some of the responsibility, especially if children were concerned. The competitors would have been misled into expecting help that was not in fact available. Again, in, for example, a transatlantic race, an inexperienced competitor might be entitled to expect that suitable safety regulations were prescribed and the boats were checked for conformity with them.

In general I believe that if it were found that a race committee had been negligent in failing to provide the safety arrangements that could reasonably be expected, or that had been promised, this rule would not prevent liability for damages.

5 Drugs

> A competitor shall neither take a substance nor use a method banned by Appendix L. An alleged breach of this rule shall not be grounds for a *protest*, and rule 63.1 does not apply.

Anyone, anywhere, who takes a prohibited substance without the permission of the ISAF International Medical Commission, and then goes racing, breaks this rule. Those tablets you took a short while ago *may* mean that you are guilty of doping without knowing it. The more pragmatic side is that since dope testing can only be initiated by a national authority or the ISAF, only the front rank of sailors are ever affected. Details are in Appendix L.

(Numbers 6–9 are spare numbers)

Part 2 – When Boats Meet

> *The rules of Part 2 apply between boats that are sailing in or near the racing area and intend to **race**, are **racing**, or have been **racing**. However, a boat not **racing** shall not be penalized for breaking one of these rules, except rule 22.1. The International Regulations for Preventing Collisions at Sea or government right-of-way rules apply between a boat sailing under these rules and a vessel that is not, and they replace these rules if the sailing instructions so state.*

Part 2 is the racing IRPCS; it tells us when the rules will be used, which boats have right of way, what restrictions are imposed on them, the obligations on give-way boats, how to get round marks and obstructions, and what to do about such awkward happenings as capsizes or anchoring. The rules of Part 2 cannot be altered by national authority prescription, by sailing instructions or by class rules (rule 86.1), but rules in Appendices B, C, D and E adapt Part 2 rules to those necessary for each specialized kind of racing. Rule 86.2 allows some experimental changes to be tried in local races.

Preamble
As well as the Part 2 rules, competitors should know the IRPCS rules – the ordinary 'rule of the road at sea' (or local government rules – for example, on the Great Lakes or the local reservoir) that boats follow when cruising. The preamble permits the substitution of Part 2 by the IRPCS, and establishes which of these two right-of-way rules will apply at any given moment.

1 Boat A, racing, meets C, a cruiser with no intention of racing: the IRPCS govern their encounter. If there is a collision and A is at fault, she will be liable just as if she were not racing. In ISAF 137, however, it is made clear that, while Part 2 rules may not apply, other rules in the book certainly do. W, racing, was required by the local government right-of-way rules to keep clear of a boat not racing to leeward of her. W intentionally hit L, bumping her boom several times and causing damage. W was disqualified under rule 11 and her appeal was dismissed. The preamble makes it clear that W was bound by the

governmental rules, but she was also bound by the racing rules other than those in Part 2. Furthermore, by intentionally hitting L, she committed a gross breach of good manners and was subject to further penalization under rule 69.

2 A and B, boats in a series, meet when they are not racing and not 'in or near the racing area'. They are not subject to the rules of Part 2 and are governed by IRPCS, but both could be disciplined under rule 69.

3 A meets B again, still before the preparatory signal, but in the racing area. Neither is racing, but both are intending to do so. The rules of Part 2 now apply, although neither boat can yet be disqualified (except under rule 69). The use of Part 2 rules in this situation is logical, for helmsmen cannot swop rules between the five- and ten-minute guns, and earlier classes in the area may already be racing. For reasons of safety, one set of rules must govern all boats close together – preferably the racing rules, which are specifically designed to deal with fleets milling around a starting line. Although the infringing boat may not yet be penalized, the right-of-way boat, if she were damaged, could protest, win her protest, and then request redress under rule 62.1(b).

4 A intends to race, but before her preparatory signal she encounters B already racing in a different class. The encounter is governed by the Part 2 rules. A will be penalized if she breaks rule 22.1, and again redress might be due to either if she was right of way and damaged.

5 Sailing instructions can prescribe that Part 2 is replaced by the IRPCS, usually at night or during trans-oceanic races. It is not mandatory to change the rules at sunset, and may not be advisable to do so in northern latitudes at midsummer or in confined waters artificially lit.

I believe that a boat that breaks an IRPCS rule, when prescribed, can still do her turns using rule 44 to exonerate herself.

Section A – Right of Way

> *A boat has right of way when another boat is required to **keep clear** of her. However, some rules in Sections B and C limit the actions of a right-of-way boat.*

Preamble

The first question in any situation is, 'Am I the keep-clear boat?' If the answer is 'yes', the second question is, 'Do the rules give me any right to room or any other rights?' If the answer to the first question is 'no', the second question is: 'Can I, as the right-of-way boat, do what I like, and if not what are my obligations?'

When *Daisy* is the right-of-way boat, the other boat, *Buttercup* (called the keep-clear or give-way boat) has to keep clear. This does not mean that *Daisy* can go barging on regardless; all her actions are governed by rules 14 and 16, some by rule 15, and there are a number of others that curtail her rights. When she gives room she is still right-of-way boat. When *Buttercup* is entitled to room she is still give-way boat, and she must keep clear except for the very limited space given to her by the definition Room.

What does 'keep clear' entail? The first phrase in the definition holds no surprises, but note that the right-of-way boat must be able to sail her course, not just her proper course, but any course she wishes to sail. There will be occasions when the right-of-way boat is restricted to her proper course, but not by this definition. The second phrase of the definition covers the situations where A overtakes B to weather and, as A's bow overlaps B's stern, they become overlapped as W and L respectively. Now L has right of way, and W must keep clear, and allow L to change course provided L does not break rules 14, 15 or 16. But if W has sailed so close to L that L cannot move, either by luffing or, if she has a long counter, by bearing away, without breaking one, or even all three, of these rules, this second phrase will put W in the wrong. (See also the definition Keep Clear.)

Rule 10 On Opposite Tacks

> When boats are on opposite *tacks*, a *port-tack* boat shall *keep clear* of a *starboard-tack* boat.

The principle of rule 10 is simple and unequivocal, yet it is a rule that generates more protests than any other. There is a considerable amount of case law to be looked at and there are a few occasions when it does not apply.

The exceptions are listed here and each is discussed under its own rule number:

1 Rule 13 states that from the time a boat passes through head to wind until she is on her new course she must keep clear, and that rule 10 does not apply. This means that while *Daisy* is tacking on to starboard, although she becomes S as she passes through head to wind, P has no obligation to keep clear of her (except to comply with rule 14).

2 In rule 18.2(b), in certain circumstances, P, when clear ahead, is under no obligation to keep clear of S and rule 10 does not apply.

3 Tacking at an obstruction under rule 19.1(b), S must give room to P and rule 10 does not apply.

4 Rule 20 lists situations where S loses her rights: returning to start, doing penalty turns, and sailing backwards.

5 S's rights may be restricted by the need to avoid capsized boats etc (rule 21) and, when not racing, by rule 22.

Turning to the case law, look at a straight 'port and starboard', an incident free from the complications of rules 13 and 16. P believes she can safely pass ahead of S and holds her course; S bears away believing she would otherwise hit P. An old US case, no longer published but still valid, concerned such an incident: S, when about 20 feet distant from P (both 8-Metre boats), bore away about 15 degrees and passed astern of P, clearing her by about 5 feet or less. The protest committee deduced that had the boats continued at the same speed on their original courses, P would have cleared S. S's protest was dismissed and she appealed.

The US Appeals Committee's remarks in reversing the decision and upholding the appeal have never been bettered: 'Had S held her course and had P crossed her, an incontrovertible fact would have been established and a protest by S would have been disallowed. But S actually bore away, and the prognostication that P would have crossed her was based on an estimate of clearance by inches, and on the constancy of the speed and course of each boat, two factors which, owing to the vagaries of the wind, are subject to rapid changes. Reasonable doubt exists as to whether P would have cleared S had the latter held her course. When there is reasonable doubt as to the ability of P to cross ahead of S, S is entitled to bear away and protest.' RYA 81/9 closely follows the old US case.

The situation is further illustrated in ISAF 113 (Fig 1) where, in a similar case, P did not deny or admit that S bore away, but said that, if she did, it was unnecessary. This was the most favourable picture P could present. Drawing heavily on the US case quoted above, the CYA stated: 'When a protest committee found that S did not alter course or that there was not a genuine and reasonable apprehension of collision on the part of S, it should have disallowed the protest. When satisfied that S did alter course and there was reasonable doubt that P could have crossed ahead of S, if S had not so altered course, then P should have been disqualified.' The case goes on to discuss rule 10 in some detail; after outlining incorrect methods of reaching decisions by some protest committees, it describes S's problems and then

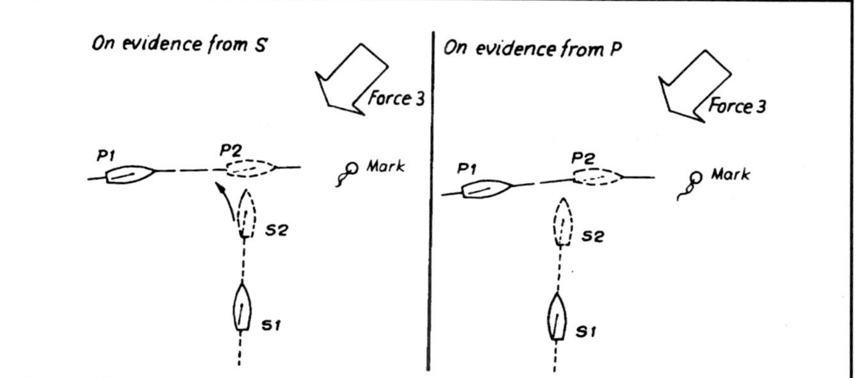

Fig 1 ISAF 113

says of P: 'P must present adequate evidence to establish either that S did not alter course or that P would have safely crossed ahead of S and that S had no need to take avoiding action.'

A recent case, ISAF 169 (Fig 56) (see definition Keep Clear), holds that P may avoid a collision and yet not keep clear.

RYA 86/1 gives P another warning: on a dark night, in force 7–8 (under RRS, not IRPCS) S and P collided, after S had taken avoiding action. P was penalized under rule 10 and appealed, maintaining that she would have passed safely astern of S had S's luff not prevented her from doing so. Dismissing P's appeal, the RYA said: 'When one boat is required to keep clear of another, the give-way boat shall, as far as possible, act clearly and early enough to ensure that the right-of-way boat is in no doubt that she is fulfilling her obligations.'

Hails are frequently exchanged between P and S; they are not required by rule 10 (or any other except rules 19 and 61.1), but in ISAF 169, for instance, had P hailed that she had heard and seen S, S would probably not have been frightened, not have headed up, and P would have passed astern of her without incident – just a common P and S crossing.

Hails such as 'hold your course' are not provided for and do not affect the operation of rule 10. In US 137, S hailed 'Starboard tack' and P, believing she could cross S, responded 'Hold your course'. S, however, tacked short and protested. In reply to P's hail it was said: 'It is permissible to hail, but the rules do not recognize such a hail as binding on the other boat. S can tack or bear away at any time she is satisfied that an alteration of course will be necessary to avoid a collision.' There is a reason for the lack of hails in the rules. A hail made clearly, heard and understood may be useful; a hail misunderstood either because of noise or because of language problems can be dangerous.

Rule 10 appears with other rules in many situations; each will be dealt with under the other rule.

Rule 11 On the Same Tack, Overlapped

> When boats are on the same *tack* and *overlapped*, a *windward* boat shall *keep clear* of a *leeward* boat.

Two same-tack boats must, by definition, be either clear ahead and clear astern of each other or overlapped. Opposite-tack boats only fall within the definition when rule 18 applies.

Overlapped or not, two same-tack boats can be on converging or parallel courses; the two may converge on steady courses or they may converge because one of them alters course – L by luffing, or W by bearing away. L's right to luff may be restricted to not above her proper course. A faster boat may establish an overlap to windward or to leeward. There may not be just two boats, but a whole row of boats. All these variables make it difficult to determine the exact facts and, even when the facts are known, sometimes difficult to apply the rule correctly.

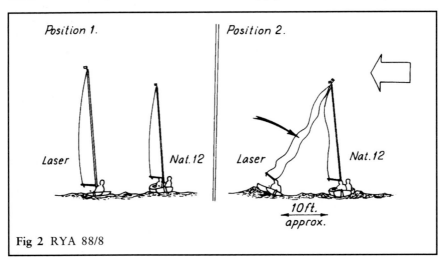

Fig 2 RYA 88/8

Rule 11 is addressed to W and always applies except while the other boat, L, is subject to rule 13 or unless modified while passing a mark or obstruction. W must keep clear, even in such a situation as that shown by RYA 88/8 (Fig 2). In this case, W was disqualified, the RYA saying: 'A leeward boat that suddenly heels to windward maintains her rights provided that her action is not deliberate.'

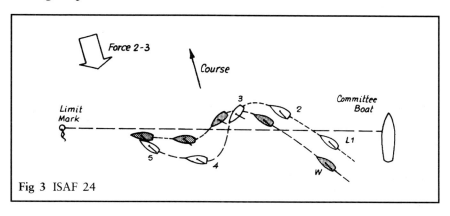

Fig 3 ISAF 24

ISAF 24 (Fig 3) shows a classic pre-start incident. L passed astern of W (position 3), overtaking her to leeward and then sailing a steady course without luffing until her shroud touched W's boom end. L protested under rule 11, W under rules 12 and 15. The protest committee found that L had right of way under rule 11 from the time she assumed a steady course until contact. W had enough room to keep clear, although she would have had to cross the starting line early to do so. Therefore, it dismissed W's protest and upheld L's. W appealed, this time citing rule 16.

Her appeal was dismissed. While rule 16 applied between positions 3 and 4, L's alteration of course to windward during that interval did not affect W. Between positions 4 and 5, while L was sailing a close-hauled course, rule 11 applied. W had enough room to keep clear, but failed to do so.

The definition Proper Course tells us what is and what is not a proper course. ISAF 106 (Fig 17) shows that a leeward boat is entitled to sail up to her proper course. W had been sailing almost dead down-wind straight towards the starboard end of the finishing line, when L overlapped her to leeward. In the absence of W, L would have sailed a higher course directly towards the line. In order to do so, she hailed W to come up. There was no response. L hailed again and luffed, but W still did not respond. L stopped luffing and there was no contact. L protested under rule 17.2.

The protest was dismissed but L, claiming the right to luff up to her proper course under rule 17.1, won her appeal. While L was not

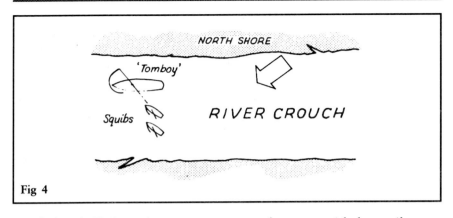

NORTH SHORE

'Tomboy'

Squibs

RIVER CROUCH

Fig 4

entitled to luff above her proper course, she was entitled to sail up to it. Accordingly, she did not exceed the limitation to which rule 17.1 subjected her. W, whether or not sailing a proper course, was therefore obligated to keep clear of L, which she failed to do, by preventing L from luffing up to her proper course. By hailing twice before luffing, L gave W room to keep clear, as required by rule 16. W was disqualified for breaking rule 11. ISAF 25 confirms this. The point is also well illustrated by an unpublished case that sticks vividly in my mind. *Tomboy* (Fig 4), a large slowish handicap cruiser, was broad-reaching up the River Crouch with the wind on her starboard quarter when two Squibs, on the same tack, chose – for perfectly legitimate reasons of wind and tide – to cross the river to the north bank. While doing so, their courses converged with *Tomboy*'s, which made no attempt to get out of their way. One of the Squibs protested her and she was disqualified under rule 11 for failing to keep clear. She is probably still wondering why.

ISAF 46 tells us that L cannot establish her overlap so close to W that poor W cannot luff to keep clear without her stern touching L. However, this does not permit W to give an unnecessary or excessive luff. (See also the definition Proper Course.)

Rule 12 On the Same Tack, Not Overlapped

> When boats are on the same *tack* and not *overlapped*, a boat *clear astern* shall *keep clear* of a boat *clear ahead*.

This rule applies to same-tack boats only. In open water, S, even though astern, will have right of way over P. At marks and obstructions, boats are governed by rule 18.2(b). Inspection of the definition Clear Astern tells us that when considering the relative positions of *Daisy* and *Buttercup,* their equipment must be in 'normal position'. *Daisy*, astern, cannot get an overlap by suddenly sticking out a spinnaker pole (if she is not going to hoist a spinnaker). Similarly, if *Buttercup*, clear ahead, loses control of her spinnaker that streams astern and then touches *Daisy*, she cannot protest *Daisy* for infringing rule 12 (ISAF 153). Certainly, since it is the right-of-way boat doing something unexpected and unpredictable, the give-way boat perhaps needs the same protection as she has against alterations of course under rule 16. But this decision is very limited. US 271 suggests that it only holds good while *Daisy* cannot see and cannot keep clear. She cannot run into equipment that has been 'out of normal position' for a long time (a spinnaker flying out of control for an entire leg). The circumstances of each case arising from these kinds of situations will need to be carefully looked at. Of course, if *Buttercup* suddenly slows down and *Daisy*'s spinnaker hits *Buttercup*'s backstay, *Daisy* will have no excuse.

ISAF 5 is discussed under rule 18.2(b).

Rule 13 While Tacking

> After a boat passes head to wind, she shall *keep clear* of other boats until she is on a close-hauled course. During that time rules 10, 11 and 12 do not apply. If two boats are subject to this rule at the same time, the one on the other's port side shall *keep clear.*

The rule does not mention the word 'tack' in any form. (Titles are not rules – see definition Rule.) Tacking is presumed to mean what everybody thinks it means, starting on starboard tack and finishing on port tack or vice versa. The rule does not apply to gybing.

'A boat that luffs head to wind and holds that point of sailing and does not pass beyond head to wind does not come within the scope of rule 13 and cannot infringe it.' This interpretation from RYA 67/1 is confirmed in ISAF 58, US 138 and, most recently, RYA 85/6. In ISAF 32, we learn that a boat is free of the obligations of rule 13 when she is on a close-hauled course regardless of her movement through the water or the sheeting of her sails.

As usual, there are exceptions:

1 An inside overlapped boat that is being given room to pass a mark must be allowed room to tack when that manoeuvre is necessary.

2 When, for reasons of safety, *Daisy* hails for room to tack, and when the other boat hails 'You tack', rule 13 does not apply.

3 A boat returning to start, doing turns, or moving astern (rule 20) must keep clear, even of another that is tacking.

ISAF 26 shows the mark rounding situation for boats that are clear astern and clear ahead of each other (rule 18.2(b)).

Finally, the rule clarifies the situation when boats tack at the same time. When two boats are subject to this rule at the same time, the one on the other's port side must keep clear. This situation can occur either when same-tack boats tack, or when the two boats tack into each other, or away from each other and their sterns hit.

Section B – General Limitations

Rules 10, 11 and 12 may give the impression that the right-of-way boat can ride roughshod over the give-way boats, but this is not so. Here are four rules that control the right-of-way boat and, hopefully, prevent her from causing damage or ruining the racing.

Rule 14 Avoiding Contact

> A boat shall avoid contact with another boat if reasonably possible. However, a right-of-way boat or one entitled to *room*
>
> (a) need not act to avoid contact until it is clear that the other boat is not *keeping clear* or giving *room*, and
>
> (b) shall not be penalized unless there is contact that causes damage.

Collisions are bad: boats are damaged, people injured, racing spoilt, and every effort must be made to avoid them. Some contact, however, is so light – two spinnakers just touching, for example – that no one calls it a collision. However, the rule does not differentiate between contact and collisions; it calls all touching 'contact'. Rule 14(b), though, implies that there is a difference; contact is to be avoided, but 'a right-of-way boat or one entitled to room . . . shall not be penalized unless there is contact that causes damage'. She may break the rule, but she will not be penalized. I will come back to this in a moment.

Daisy must avoid contact with another boat 'if reasonably possible' even when she has right of way. Many people's reaction to this is to

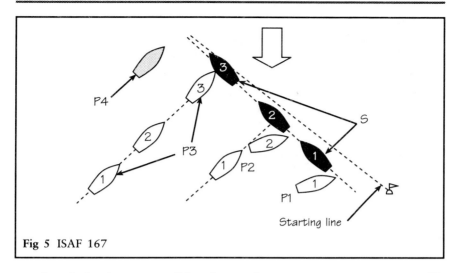

Fig 5 ISAF 167

say 'but it is always *possible*, she need not come out to race at all'. Rule 14(a) recognizes this, for she need not do anything until it is clear that the other boat, the give-way boat, is not keeping clear or giving room as she ought to. ISAF 167 (Fig 5) illustrates that a right-of-way boat need not anticipate that the other boat will not keep clear. The angle of the starting line made it only just possible for a close-hauled boat on starboard tack to cross the line, and most boats approached on port tack. However, S came in from the right-hand end, continually hailing 'Starboard'. P1 and P2 bore off below S. P3, however, made no attempt to avoid S and struck her amidships at right angles, causing considerable damage. At the last moment, when S realized that P3 was not going to keep clear, she altered course to try to minimize the impact of the collision. The protest committee disqualified both boats: P3 under rule 10, and S under rule 14. S appealed.

Reinstating S, the US Appeals Committee said: 'S was required by rule 14 to avoid contact if it was "reasonably possible" to do so. However, the second sentence of rule 14 allowed S to sail her course in the expectation that P3 would keep clear as required, until such time as it became evident that P3 would not do so. The diagram shows that P3 could readily have borne off and avoided S from a position very close to S. For that reason, the time between the moment it became evident that P3 would not keep clear and the time of the collision was a very brief interval, so brief that it was impossible for S to avoid contact. Therefore S did not break rule 14.'

(Looking back for a moment at the old rules, we have arrived at something very like old rule 32, but with damage instead of serious damage. In theory, there is the difference that the right-of-way boat in the old rule was allowed to hit another, while now she is not allowed to, but is not penalized for her infringement.)

What then is 'damage'? An attempt is made to define it in ISAF 36, where it is suggested that a series of questions should be asked. Examples are:

1 Was the current market value of any part of the boat, or of the boat as a whole, diminished?

2 Was any item of the boat or her equipment made less functional?

3 Was a member of the crew injured?

So, if you feel you could have done more to avoid a collision, and if you think that maybe there has been some damage, do your turns; having broken a rule of Part 2, exoneration under rule 44 is open to you, unless sailing instructions say otherwise.

It is not clear if the 'damage' in rule 14 is the same as the 'damage' in rule 62 (Redress), but certainly in many cases it will be.

Finally, remember that 'serious damage' can still lead to disqualification under rule 44.

Rule 14 also applies to the keep-clear boat, but not its two clauses (a) and (b) unless she is entitled to room.

In an odd case, RYA 85/7, two boats were running along a shore in light winds; although A hailed her not to do so, B forced a passage between A and the shore, and when A saw that a collision was imminent, she hailed B to pull in her boom. B did not, and her boom end hit A's backstay and brought down the mast. The RYA considered that, in the circumstances, A's hail had constituted a reasonable attempt to avoid the collision. Today, B might have been considered to have broken rule 14.

In RYA 75/4, when the right-of-way boat's helmsman was inexperienced, it was held: 'The test of the reasonableness of the attempt by S to avoid a collision resulting in damage must be an objective one. The inexperience of helmsman or crew cannot justify a lower standard of care.'

The right-of-way boat cannot always invoke the unexpectedness of the accident. In ISAF 51 (Fig 13), two boats in different classes were rounding the same mark in opposite directions. P's claim to room under rule 18 was dismissed and she was disqualified under rule 10, but S was also thrown out for failing to make a reasonable attempt to avoid a collision.

The dilemma of the right-of-way boat in choosing between rules 14 and 16 is discussed under rule 16.

Rule 15 Acquiring Right of Way

> When a boat acquires right of way, she shall initially give the other boat *room* to *keep clear*, unless she acquires right of way because of the other boat's actions.

The rule covers the boat that has just tacked on to starboard, established a leeward overlap, or – sometimes – completed penalty turns, returned to start, or stopped sailing backwards.

When she becomes the right-of-way boat, *Daisy* cannot claim her rights as soon as she gets them. She must allow the newly obligated boat room to keep clear; and it will be seen from the definition Room that it encompasses the idea of both space and time. No anticipation by the new give-way boat is expected: she does not have to guess what *Daisy* is going to do. This is expressed clearly in ISAF 53, which we have just looked at. 'While it was obvious that L would have to tack round the mark, W was under no obligation to anticipate that she would do so.' RYA 93/5 confirms this.

As one inch of *Daisy*'s bow crosses the line abeam from *Buttercup*'s stern, she becomes overlapped (see definition Clear-astern etc). When this overlap is established to leeward, *Daisy* immediately ceases to be the give-way boat and becomes the right-of-way boat (subject to rule 17.1). However, it would be unfair if W could be disqualified for failing to keep clear in that instant, for she could not do so and, as we have seen, she is not expected to anticipate. *Daisy* must initially allow W room to keep clear. W must be able to keep clear; L must not creep in so close that W cannot luff away without hitting her. If the best way for W to keep clear is to luff head to wind, then she is entitled to do so and L must give her room (ISAF 46). Equally, W may be prevented by objects to weather of her from making room, but in this case W will, except at a starting mark, have protection from rule 18 as inside boat at an obstruction.

The word 'initially' in rule 15 tells us that W must make room at the first opportunity; however, the opportunity, it has often been said, is not a continuing one. In US 233 (Fig 6), after L had established her overlap, the two boats continued sailing for a few lengths on parallel courses with L moving somewhat faster. When the boats were overlapped 8–10 feet, L, by hail, indicated her intention to luff. W responded by luffing and tacking, her port counter hitting L amidships. From the time of the overlap until after the contact, L held a steady course and did not luff. W was disqualified under rule 11. The few lengths that the two boats had sailed overlapped had been

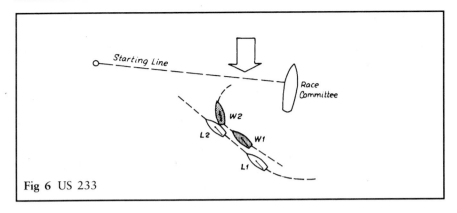

Fig 6 US 233

adequate to meet the requirements of rule 15. W, in the course of her appeal, contended: 'The leeward boat had the obligation to leave room, and room that was sufficient to satisfy the windward boat'; she maintained that the rules did not place any obligation on W during a transitional period to hold her course or luff slowly, and that rule 15 explicitly placed all the burdens on L. Dismissing her appeal, the US Appeals Committee said: 'A windward boat's right to "room" under rule 15 is a shield and not a sword for W.'

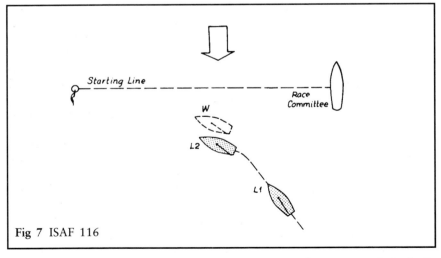

Fig 7 ISAF 116

In ISAF 116 (Fig 7), W had no way on, and in spite of L's hails did nothing until L was overlapped, when she began to trim sails and head up. The protest committee disqualified W because she had been given adequate warning, but had failed to keep clear. W appealed, and the US Appeals Committee reinstated her, saying: '. . . rule 15 does not require a boat clear ahead to anticipate her requirement to keep clear as a windward boat before the boat clear astern establishes an overlap to leeward'.

There is an exception in the last sentence of the rule: *Daisy*, if she becomes right-of-way boat because of *Buttercup*'s actions, need not give the initial room. This might arise, for example, where both boats are on starboard tack and *Buttercup*, ahead, suddenly tacks, and as she goes through head to wind becomes subject to rule 13, while *Daisy*, up to weather, equally suddenly becomes right-of-way boat. Unsurprisingly, *Daisy* need not give *Buttercup* room, although of course she is always subject to rule 14.

Rule 16 Changing Course

> When a right-of-way boat changes course, she shall give the other boat *room* to *keep clear*.

There are two qualifications to be fulfilled before a boat is capable of breaking rule 16: she must be right-of-way boat and she must change course. Neither an alteration of course by a give-way boat nor a right-of-way boat sailing a straight course will activate the rule. The object of rule 16 is safety. When the give-way boat – be she P, W or another – is doing her duty and keeping clear, she must not be obstructed by changes of course by the right-of-way boat. When such a change results in a collision it is usually pretty obvious that the burdened boat has been prevented from keeping clear, but when the boats do not touch the decision is more difficult. There is no exception to rule 16.

US 172 states that altering course means changing compass direction, so a boat sailing a circle is changing course continually.

I find it interesting that the rule is not unlike IRPCS Rule 17, *Action by a Stand-on Vessel*: 'Where one of two vessels is to keep out of the way, the other shall keep her course and speed.' The wind may accelerate or slow down a sailing boat at random, so the speed clause cannot be included in the racing rules. Both rules leave *Daisy*, when she is right-of-way boat, in a dilemma: rule 16 tells her that she must not change course without giving the other boat a chance to get out of the way, which perhaps she cannot do, while rule 14 forbids her to cause a collision. So *Daisy* may hold her course until it is evident that *Buttercup* is not keeping clear or giving room when *Daisy* becomes subject to rule 14 and must try to avoid the collision. The problem is illustrated by RYA 91/4, where S, a Mustang, hailed P, a J24, three times, but P took no action until it was too late. When she bore away she hit S, although the latter made a tardy and useless effort to keep clear. S had to retire, and was later disqualified under rule 14 for not having tacked off earlier. S appealed, saying that a J24 was very manoeuvrable; it was only at a very late stage that it became clear that P was not taking sufficient action; that the faces of the crew were clearly visible so that she had reason to believe P was aware of the situation; and that the conditions were not such as to cause loss of control by either boat. S was justified in taking avoiding action, in spite of rule 16 when it was clear that P was not keeping clear. S was reinstated.

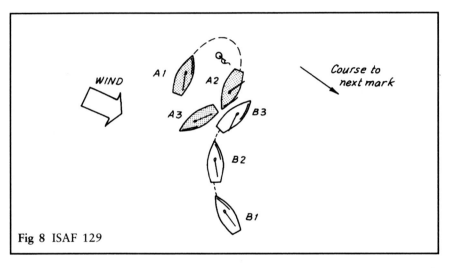

Fig 8 ISAF 129

There is a great deal of case law to be looked at in detail, starting with ISAF 129 (Fig 8). A passed the windward mark to starboard ahead of B and chose, for tactical reasons, to sail high above the next mark. To do so she gybed and luffed sharply, coming bow to bow with B. The two passed very close but without contact. The protest committee allowed A's protest under rule 10, and B appealed, alleging that A had broken rule 16 by failing to give B sufficient room to keep clear. B was reinstated on appeal. A was free to adopt any course she chose to reach the leeward mark, but she had no right to luff abruptly into B's path. Although no collision took place, A's extreme and unexpected change of course failed to give B the room that was her due.

US 186 (Fig 9) provides an excellent example of the sort of incident that rule 16 is designed to avoid. It was blowing 35 knots and gusting to 45 knots when A, a 42-foot cutter under headsail only, reached

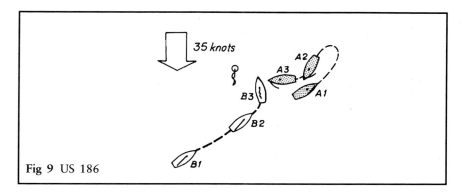

Fig 9 US 186

the mark with B, a Cal-29, with a small jib and reefed main, about 3–6 lengths astern. When A tacked, she bore away to gain speed and then hardened up to a course to clear the mark. Meanwhile B, which had seen A bearing down on her, tacked too, and A struck her full amidships causing major hull damage. When A's tack was completed she was no longer subject to rule 13 and she became the right-of-way starboard-tack boat. She was entitled to sail any course she liked, except that she could not then alter course in such a way that she defeated B's efforts to keep clear.

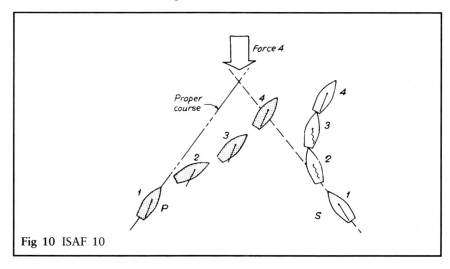

Fig 10 ISAF 10

The distance between the boats is very important. In ISAF 10 (Fig 10), P and S were close-hauled on converging courses. P bore away to pass astern of S, and a moment later S elected to tack. P resumed her close-hauled course and sailed past S about a length to windward of her. S protested under rule 16 but was disqualified; she appealed and was reinstated. 'S was subject to rule 16 while luffing from a close-hauled course to head to wind. During that time P had room to keep clear and was not compelled to change course. Once beyond head to wind, S did not have right of way over P and so rule 16 did not apply.'

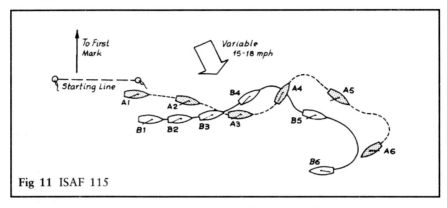

Fig 11 ISAF 115

Rule 16 protests arise most frequently before the start, when there is no proper course and changes of course are unpredictable and often continuous. In ISAF 115 (Fig 11), A is trying to drive B away from the starting line in the pre-start manoeuvres just before the starting gun. Each protested the other but, after going to appeal, the outcome was that neither had broken a rule and neither was disqualified. This case is worth looking at in detail.

Before the starting signal, A and B reached away from the line. A, sailing faster, passed and was clear ahead of B by position 3. At position 4, A luffed up to close-hauled, intending to tack back to the line, but found that B had also luffed and worked into a position where, had A tacked, there would have been an immediate collision. A then bore away to gybe, only to discover that B had now borne away into a position where a gybe would again cause a collision. Finally, B gybed and headed for the starting line, leaving A well astern. A protested B under rule 16; B was disqualified and appealed. Reversing the decision and reinstating B, the US Appeals Committee said: 'B's actions describe a classic manoeuvre in match and team racing, used to gain a favourable starting position ahead of another competitor. The essential point is that rule 16 applies only to the right-of-way boat, which B, at positions 3 and 4, was not. At position 4, B, as windward boat, had to keep clear under rule 11, but A could not tack without breaking rule 13. At position 5, B became the leeward

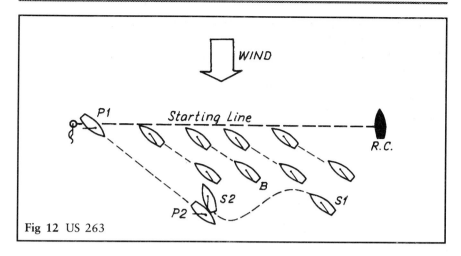

Fig 12 US 263

boat; she then began to hold rights under rule 11, and any gybe would have been subject to rules 15 and 16. The facts show that neither boat broke any rule.'

US 263 (Fig 12) warns the give-way boat that she is over-optimistic if she thinks that rule 16 is going to protect her when she has been rash. After an incident at the start in a 20 knot breeze, S protested under rule 10 and P claimed the protection of rule 16. 'While P intended to keep clear of all starboard-tack boats, she was under the assumption that they were all close-hauled ... Apparently, P was surprised when S appeared reaching from behind the other boats. The fact that P was unable to see S until they were on a collision course cannot be used to relieve her of her obligation to the right-of-way boat. The situation is not unlike one in which P barely clears S only to find another starboard tacker to windward of the one she has just cleared. In a blind situation the obligated boat must be the one to anticipate what might appear from the other side of an obstruction.'

In ISAF 35, two boats were running on opposite tacks. About two minutes after one of these had gybed on to starboard, S hailed P and began to luff. The boats touched. Did rule 10 apply or rule 16? The answer of the USSRYRF was as follows: 'S, having completed her gybe, is the right-of-way boat under rule 10, and P, as the give-way boat, is bound to keep clear.' Rule 15 applies only briefly after S becomes right-of-way boat. After that, she may luff provided she complies with rule 16.

In ISAF 51 (Fig 13), S and P, in separate races, approached the same mark on opposite tacks. Unknown to P, which was lowering her spinnaker and hardening up to round the mark to port, S was required

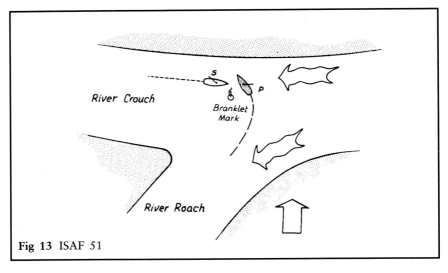

Fig 13 ISAF 51

to round it to starboard. P heard no hail and was unaware of S's presence until P's crew saw S a few yards away. He shouted a warning and leaped out of the way just as S's bow sliced through P's hull behind the mast. P protested S under rule 14 on the grounds that S could have avoided the collision. S, protesting under rule 10, claimed that, had she changed course, she would have broken rule 16. The protest committee disqualified P under rule 10. P appealed.

Dismissing the appeal, the RYA said: 'P failed to keep a proper look out and to observe her primary duty to keep clear. She is correctly disqualified under rule 10. One purpose of the rules of Part 2 is to avoid contacts between boats racing. All boats, whether or not holding right of way, should keep a look out at all times. When a boat has the opportunity to avoid a collision she must make a reasonable attempt to do so. When she does not, she breaks rule 14. When the two conflict, rule 14 overrides rule 16, and when the right-of-way boat finds herself so close that collision cannot be avoided by the action of the give-way boat alone, she is entitled to take such action under rule 14 as best will avoid damage. Since S made no attempt to avoid a collision, and damage, indeed serious damage, resulted, she is disqualified under rule 14.' In this case, the racing rules and IRPCS come very close together. ISAF 87 gives a view of changing course (and of overtaking) under the IRPCS.

Rule 17 On the Same Tack; Proper Course

17.1 A boat that establishes a *leeward overlap* from *clear astern* within two of her hull lengths of a *windward* boat shall not sail above her *proper course* during that *overlap* while the boats are less than that distance apart, unless as a result she becomes *clear astern*.

17.2 Except on a beat to windward, while a boat is less than two of her hull lengths from a *leeward* boat or a boat *clear astern* steering a course to *leeward* of her, she shall not sail below her *proper course* unless she gybes.

Since there is no proper course before the starting signal, this rule does not apply until then (see definition Proper Course), and a boat above close-hauled need not begin to bear away to her close-hauled proper course until that moment.

Rule 17.1

'A boat that establishes a *leeward overlap* from *clear astern* . . .' Consider the commonest case: A to leeward overtakes B from astern, and as her bow crosses the line of B's stern they become L and W respectively. There are other ways in which they can become L and W: they can be P and S, and one of them tacks, or A can overtake to windward, but neither of these methods will bring this rule into force.

'. . . within two of her hull lengths of a *windward* boat . . .' In addition to crossing the line across W's stern, L must cross it within two of *her* hull lengths. Fig 14 shows the situation with two same-size boats and two of different sizes.

'. . . shall not sail above her *proper course* . . .' L is restricted and cannot luff, unless her proper course changes.

'. . . while the boats are less than that distance apart . . .' The restriction lasts until L sails out of the two-length distance. Then she is free to sail above her proper course if she so wishes until she re-enters what might be thought of as a two-boat length strip alongside W, when L is again subject to rule 17.1. Of course, rule 17.1 ends as soon as L gets clear ahead or drops back and becomes clear astern.

'. . . unless as a result she becomes *clear astern*.' It would be unfair to pin L down if she wants to luff without worrying W, so this last phrase allows her to luff provided this luff brings her clear astern of W, leaving L free to luff further, or tack if she wants to.

ISAF 25 (Fig 15) (discussed under 'Proper Course') states that when, owing to a difference of opinion about a leeward boat's proper course,

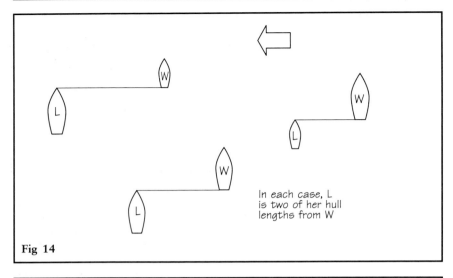

Fig 14

In each case, L is two of her hull lengths from W

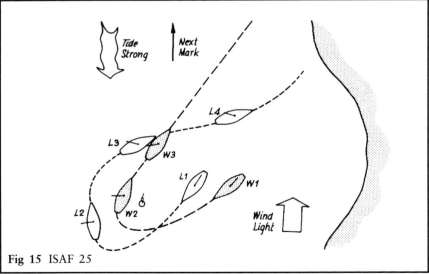

Fig 15 ISAF 25

two boats on the same tack converge, the windward boat must keep clear and that there can be more than one proper course.

In ISAF 11 (Fig 16), L established a leeward overlap on W from clear astern about 200 yards from the mark. L was less than two of her hull lengths from W. The two boats then sailed alongside each other, about one-and-a-half lengths apart, until they were 80 yards

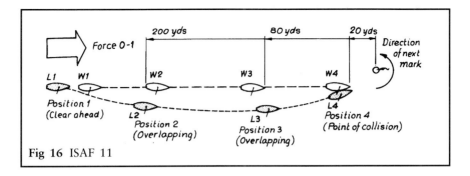

Fig 16 ISAF 11

from the mark. At this point, L began to luff up slightly to lay the mark. W, not sailing below her proper course, maintained a steady course. L never became clear ahead. W's boom touched L's shroud, although without damage, and L protested under rule 11, but she was disqualified on the grounds that she had not allowed W enough room to fulfil her obligation to keep clear as required by rule 15. L's appeal was upheld, with the US Appeals Committee stating: 'When L established a leeward overlap from clear astern, W became bound by rule 11 to keep clear of L. At the same time, L was bound by rule 15 to allow W room to keep clear, but that obligation is not a continuing one, and in this case the overlap had been in existence for a considerable period during which nothing had obstructed W's room.

'L was justified in altering course to approach the mark, provided that she did not sail above her proper course; it is L's proper course that is the criterion for deciding whether W broke rule 11 or L broke rule 17.1. L at no time sailed above her proper course; the facts indicate that she gave W room as rule 16 required. W is disqualified under rule 11, and L is reinstated.'

In ISAF 106 (Fig 17), the following events occurred. For some time W had been sailing almost dead downwind straight towards the starboard end of the finishing line, when L overlapped her to leeward. L wanted to come up, twice hailed W to come up, and then luffed. There was no response, so L stopped luffing without contact. L protested under rule 17.2. The protest committee held that there was insufficient evidence to show that W would have finished sooner by sailing a higher course; therefore she did not break rule 17.2 by sailing below her proper course. Even though there might be conflict between the courses of a windward and a leeward boat, it said, a boat overtaking another from clear astern did not have the right to force a windward boat to sail above her proper course. The protest was dismissed and L appealed, claiming the right to luff up to her proper course under rule 17.1.

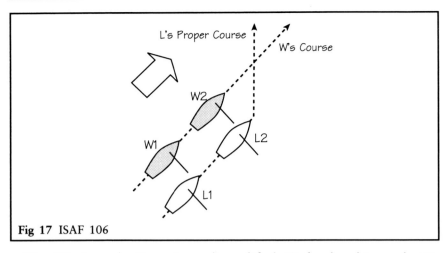

Fig 17 ISAF 106

The US Appeals Committee disqualified W for breaking rule 11, saying that 'rule 11 says that, when two boats on the same tack are overlapped, W shall keep clear. L's actions, however, are limited by rules 16 and 17.1. In this case, by hailing twice before luffing, L gave W room to keep clear, as required by rule 16. The protest committee, although it did not say so explicitly, recognized that L's proper course was directly toward the finishing line. A direct course to the line was not only closer but would also have put both boats on a faster point of sailing. While L was not entitled to luff above her proper course, she was entitled to sail up to it. Accordingly, she did not exceed the limitation to which rule 17.1 subjected her. W, whether or not sailing a proper course, had therefore to keep clear of L, which she failed to do, by preventing L from sailing up to her proper course.'

Rule 17.2

The boats are still on the same tack, and the rule is still about limitations on sailing below or above a proper course. While 17.1 controlled L, 17.2 controls the other boat, which may be W or the boat clear ahead. Notice that the rule does not apply on the wind; it is an off-the-wind rule.

The rule is often spoken of as if it prevented W (as we will call her, but remember she may be clear ahead) from bearing away, but in fact it only prevents her from sailing 'below her proper course'. In US 79 (Fig 18), W, because of a strong current and a light wind, headed to leeward of the direct line to the mark, a course that in fact brought her directly to it. The fact that W did not sail straight for the mark did not mean she was sailing below her proper course.

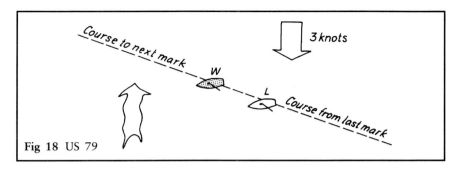

Fig 18 US 79

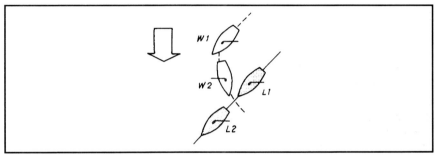

Fig 19 W may bear away provided she gybes.

Fig 19 shows how the last phrase of rule 17.2 permits W to gybe and cross L's stern without infringing it.

Rule C2.2 deletes rule 17.2 for match racing; rule D1.1(e) permits sailing instructions to alter rule 17.2 for team racing.

Section C – At Marks and Obstructions

When a Section C rule applies, the rules in Sections A and B continue to apply unless the Section C rule modifies them or states that they do not apply.

Preamble
Note: I shall use 'mark' for 'mark and obstruction' unless a rule specifically applies to one only, and I shall refer to the defined term 'two-length zone' as 'the circle'. The preamble warns us not to throw away the rules we have looked at so far just because we have arrived at a mark; Section C tells us when they are cancelled or modified.

Rule 18 Passing Marks and Obstructions

18.1 When this rule applies

Rule 18 applies at a *mark* or *obstruction* to be left on the same side when boats are about to pass it, until they have passed it. However, it does not apply

(a) at a starting *mark* or its anchor line surrounded by navigable water from the time the boats are approaching them to *start* until they have passed them, or

(b) between boats on opposite *tacks* when they are on a beat to windward or when the *proper course* for one of them to pass the *mark* or *obstruction* is to tack.

18.2 Giving Room; Keeping Clear

(a) When boats are *overlapped* before one of them reaches the *two-length zone*, if the outside boat has right of way she shall give the inside boat *room* to pass the *mark* or *obstruction*, or if the inside boat has right of way the outside boat shall *keep clear*. If they are still *overlapped* when one of them reaches the *two-length zone*, the outside boat's obligation continues even if the *overlap* is broken later. This rule does not apply if the outside boat is unable to give *room* when the *overlap* begins.

(b) If a boat is *clear ahead* when she reaches the *two-length zone*, the boat *clear astern* shall *keep clear* even if an *overlap* is established later. Rule 10 does not apply. If the boat *clear ahead* tacks, rule 13 applies and this rule no longer does.

(c) If there is reasonable doubt that a boat established or broke an *overlap* in time, it shall be presumed that she did not.

18.3 Tacking

If two boats were on opposite *tacks* and one of them tacked within the *two-length zone* to pass a *mark* or *obstruction*, rule 18.2 does not apply. The boat that tacked

(a) shall not cause the other boat to sail above close-hauled to avoid her or prevent the other boat from passing the *mark* or *obstruction*, and

(b) shall *keep clear* if the other boat becomes *overlapped* inside her, in which case rule 15 does not apply.

18.4 Gybing

When rule 18.2(a) applies and an inside *overlapped* right-of-way boat must gybe at the *mark* or *obstruction* to sail her *proper course*, she shall pass no farther from the *mark* or *obstruction* than needed to sail that course.

18.5   Passing a Continuing Obstruction

At a continuing *obstruction*, rule 18.2 is modified so that while boats are passing the *obstruction* an outside boat's obligation ends if the *overlap* is broken, and a boat *clear astern* may establish an inside *overlap* provided there is *room* at that time to pass between the other boat and the *obstruction*. If she does so, her obligation under rule 18.2(b) ends.

Rule 18.1 When Rule 18 Applies (and when it doesn't)

'. . . at a *mark* or *obstruction* . . .' The meaning of these defined terms is discussed under 'definitions'.

'. . . to be left on the same side . . .' The use of the words 'to be left' implies that the boats must pass on one side, either because sailing instructions require the mark to be left to port by both boats or, in the case of an obstruction, because it can only be left on one side. ISAF 51 (Fig 13), described under rule 14, shows a case where different classes were sent different ways round the same mark, and rule 18 did not apply.

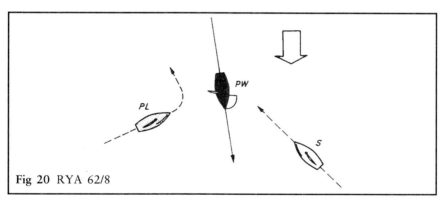

Fig 20 RYA 62/8

'On the same side' must, I believe, refer to port or starboard; if sailing instructions only say 'pass to the north of buoy X', P and S can both pass to the north yet leave the mark on different sides. RYA 62/8 (Fig 20) states that rule 18 does not apply when two boats are passing an obstruction but not, or not necessarily, on the same side. PW, running on port, caused PL, close-hauled on port, to alter course to avoid a collision. PW left the obstruction, S, on her port side; had PL not been forced to tack it was probable that she would have passed ahead of S, leaving S on her starboard side. PW was disqualified under rule 11 and appealed on the ground that the protest committee had failed to take into account her rights under rule 18. Dismissing the appeal, the RYA said: 'The conditions for the application of rule 18.1 were not satisfied; PL and PW were not necessarily about to leave S on the same side, and PW was correctly disqualified.'

'. . . about to pass . . .' This 'has never been defined precisely,' ISAF 163 states, 'nor can it be. In approaching a mark there is no exact point at which a boat becomes "about to pass it". Almost always a boat two lengths from a mark is about to pass it, but this is sometimes so at a greater distance too . . . the nearer the boat is to the mark the more definitely she is about to pass it.'

Imagine running at 8 knots with a spinnaker in force 5 with a 2-knot tide under you; in a 6-Metre boat you will take just 2.4 seconds to reach the mark from the edge of the circle. Reason tells you that you were 'about to pass' earlier. Alternatively, if that 2-knot tide was against you in a flattish calm you might *never* be about to pass. However, for ordinary everyday purposes, the circle is considered the vital moment when the rule changes.

'. . . until they have passed it . . .' The circle ceases to have any function once adequate room has been given, meaning that rule 18 does not continue to govern until the boats are out of the circle. The rule refers to 'they', so both boats must be clear of the mark or obstruction. There is no cut and dried rule; that *Daisy* is on her new course is not necessarily evidence that she has completed her rounding, for the tide may well keep her stationary although heading in the right direction. But once past, the right-of-way boat that has had to give room recovers her full rights immediately. She is only subject to rules 14 and 16. As was said in US 12, '. . . rule 18.2 makes an exception to rule 11 only so far as to require the outside boat, although holding right of way, to give the inside boat room to round safely and clear the mark'. ISAF 50 (Fig 21) shows two dinghies passing a mark. L, outside, gave room to W to pass and then, one length beyond the

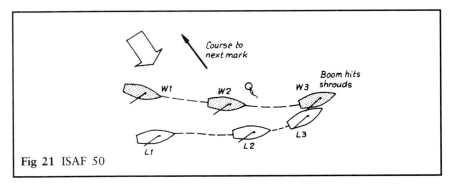

Fig 21 ISAF 50

mark, began to luff towards the next mark. W was slow to head up and the boats touched. W was disqualified and failed in her appeal. Both boats had passed the mark and W had not been prevented from keeping clear because of her proximity to the mark.

RYA 69/7 tells us about W having an inside overlap on L. After luffing round the mark together, W either bore away slightly or was a little slow in hardening her main sheet, and the boats touched. This happened when they were about level, sailing close-hauled away from the mark and about one and a half lengths from it. The protest committee decided that W was still in the act of passing the mark and disqualified L for not giving enough room. L appealed and was reinstated (W being disqualified), the RYA saying: 'Bearing in mind the conditions of wind and current, a boat that has left a mark one and a half lengths astern is no longer in the act of passing it. Rule 18 has ceased to apply.' RYA 90/4 and 90/6 also deal with incidents when the boats were held to be clear of the marks and rule 18 no longer applied. Rule 18 does not apply in two sets of circumstances: at starting marks and between opposite-tack boats on a beat.

Rule 18.1(a) At Starting Marks '. . . a starting *mark* or its anchor line surrounded by navigable water . . .' (I think it should be a starting mark *and* its anchor line, since you are unlikely to meet an unattached anchor line!) This includes the committee boat (even though it is an obstruction), the pin end mark and any outer or inner distance marks when they are laid.

'. . . from the time the boats are approaching them to *start* until they have passed them . . .' This means the period from your run up to the line until you are over it and clear of the mark. L is always

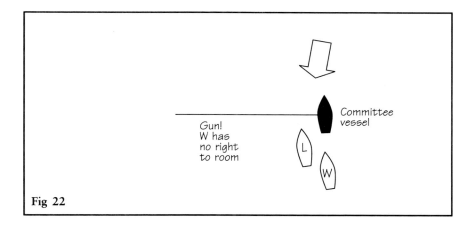

Gun!
W has
no right
to room

Committee
vessel

Fig 22

subject to rule 16 so she cannot luff W into the committee boat without giving her room to keep clear, but she can sail a straight steady course which will not let W in and will force her to go the wrong side of the committee boat (Fig 22).

Rule 18.1(b) Boats on Opposite Tacks This rule has wide application – its most obvious being when two close-hauled opposite-tack boats arrive at the windward mark at the end of the beat; in this instance, rule 10 governs their relationship, not rule 18. As soon as they become same-tack boats, rule 18 comes into force.

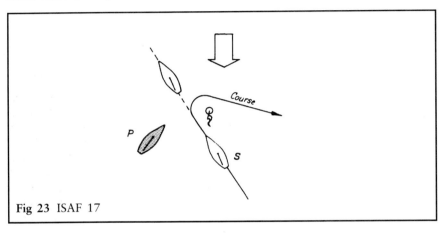

Fig 23 ISAF 17

In ISAF 17 (Fig 23), S and P meet at a starboard-hand windward mark. S can tack and round the mark; but instead of tacking, S holds her course with the intention of forcing P to tack to keep clear. The question was asked: 'Can P disregard rule 10 if she considers S to be sailing beyond her proper course and to have sufficient room to round the mark?' 'No,' came back the answer from the RYA, 'rule 10 applies. In accordance with rule 18.1(b) the boats are not subject to rule 18, thus when S chooses to hold her course, P must keep clear.'

Similarly, in RYA 81/3 (Fig 24) A was disqualified after an appeal by B. The protest committee applied rule 18.2(b) wrongly. A had been clear ahead of B two lengths from the mark and remained right-of-way boat (even if she gybed or B got an overlap inside the circle) unless she tacked. When A tacked on to port she was required to comply with rule 13 and when she tried to cross ahead of B, on starboard tack, she became subject to rule 10, exactly as she would have been had the mark not been there.' ISAF 159 makes the same point.

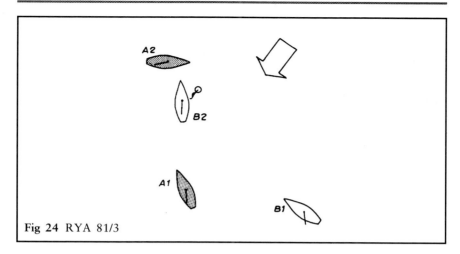

Fig 24 RYA 81/3

The consequences of the unavailability of rule 18 to boats on a beat can be seen at obstructions as well as at marks, as illustrated by ISAF 93 (Fig 25). P can just lay along the shore, while S, which for some undisclosed reason has been further offshore, now comes in. P has neither the protection of rule 18, because of the exception we are considering, nor of rule 19.1, which is only available to same-tack boats. P *must* keep clear. A close-hauled port-tack boat that is sailing parallel and close to a continuing obstruction must be prepared to keep clear of a boat that has completed her tack to starboard and is approaching on a collision course. Note that the only way starboard can pass the obstruction is by tacking, thus satisfying the requirement of rule 18.1(b). Such incidents are common and RYA 84/11 shows another.

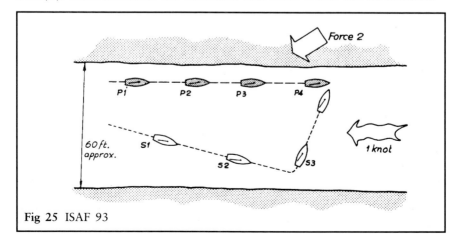

Fig 25 ISAF 93

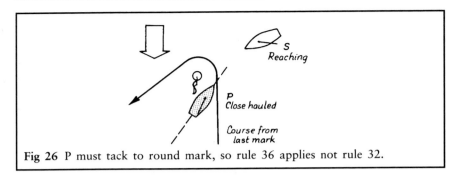

Fig 26 P must tack to round mark, so rule 36 applies not rule 32.

Sometimes one of the two opposite-tack boats overstands so far that she is no longer close-hauled as she comes to the mark, but P will have to tack to pass the mark (Fig 26) so the requirements of the section are fulfilled. Finally, remember that we are dealing only with tacking; at the gybe mark, rule 18 applies in full.

Rule 18.2 *Giving Room; Keeping Clear*
This rule contains the instructions for *Daisy* to get past marks without running into other boats and having to do endless turns or being disqualified. Rule E3 alters the two-length zone to a four-length zone for radio-controlled boat racing.

Rule 18.2(a) *Daisy* and *Buttercup* have been overlapped all the way down the leg, and now, unless *Daisy* can get clear ahead of *Buttercup* before they reach the circle, *Daisy* must keep clear or give room as is appropriate.

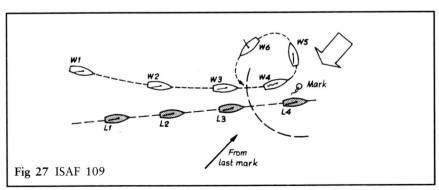

Fig 27 ISAF 109

There are two situations; in the first, the outside boat, *Daisy*, has right of way (she is either S or L). She must give *Buttercup* room to

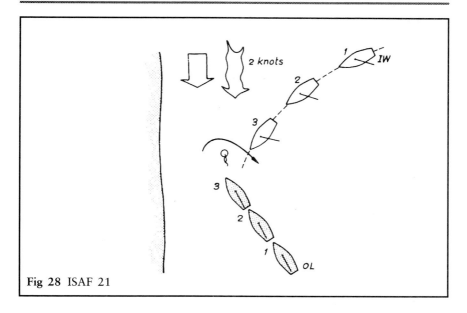

Fig 28 ISAF 21

pass, and here room will include a tack or a gybe when necessary. ISAF 109 (Fig 27) shows what happens when the outside boat does not give enough room. L and W were overlapped at the circle, but L left no room for W which had to go the wrong side of the mark. L was disqualified. (The case is printed because of its interpretation of rule 63.2; it merely illustrates rule 18.2(a).) ISAF 21 (Fig 28) shows another L trying to keep W out, but in vain; W is overlapped and has her rights under rule 18.2(a).

But, unless she is keeping clear of *Daisy*, *Buttercup* must not take more room than she needs; she must manoeuvre promptly in a seamanlike way (see definition Room) and must not try a tactical rounding if it means her taking more room than was really necessary.

ISAF 145 (Fig 29) shows W with her coveted inside position at the mark, but she has been too greedy in trying to take more room than she needed, and so got herself disqualified under rule 11. Upholding the protest committee's decision, the US Appeals Committee said: 'The diagram accepted by the committee showed both L and W on courses leading them to leeward of the mark with adequate room for W to round it. The relationship between rules 11 and 18.2(a) is defined by the Preamble to Section C of Part 2. In this incident, rule 11 did not cease to apply; it continued to obligate W to keep clear of L unless she was prevented from doing so by L's failure to give her sufficient room. Although rule 18 applied, because the boats were "about to

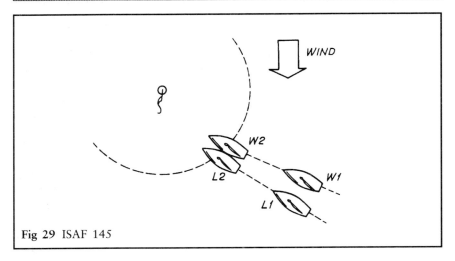

Fig 29 ISAF 145

pass" the mark, and rule 18.2(a) gave W the right to the room she needed to pass it, the fact was that she already had this room before and at the time of contact. The boats were within the two-length zone, but this did not give W any additional rights. She therefore broke rule 11 by failing to keep clear of L.' US 119 confirms this.

In the second situation, *Daisy* is the keep-clear boat, either W or P. If the passing involves a gybe, *Buttercup* is constrained by rule 18.4 to gybe, if the boats are on the same tack and *Buttercup* established the overlap from astern, then she will be constrained by rule 17.1 not to sail above her proper course. If neither of these rules applies, *Buttercup* can carry *Daisy* off as far as she likes. ISAF 166 shows a

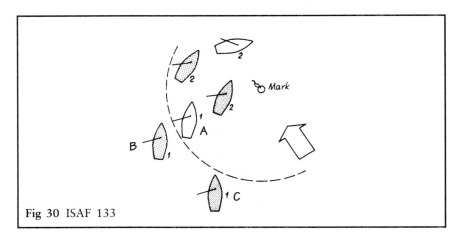

Fig 30 ISAF 133

tactical rounding by the inside leeward boat where she sailed some way from the mark but always on her proper course.

When the outside boat voluntarily or unintentionally makes room available to another that has no rights to such room and does not make or indicate any claim to it, the inside boat can take advantage, at her own risk, of the room so given. ISAF 133 (Fig 30) shows three boats approaching a mark on a run. A and B were overlapped with B outside and C further astern. A and B rounded, leaving ample room for C to pass inside. B, because of her position outside A, was unable to luff C and at no time sailed a course that would have resulted in a collision with her. There was no collision. B protested C for taking room she had no right to, but her protest and appeal were dismissed. C broke no rule, nor did B suffer any disadvantage from C's rounding of the mark. ISAF 127 (Fig 31) shows us five boats nearing a leeward mark, four overlapped, such that the two outside boats are pushed outside the circle. The fifth, coming up from astern, gains an overlap when the others gybe and is entitled to room from the two that had not reached the circle.

Rule 18.2(b) *Daisy* leads *Buttercup* on a reach or a run from one mark to the next. When she reaches the circle, she is still clear ahead of *Buttercup*; now *Buttercup* must keep clear of *Daisy*, even if she is

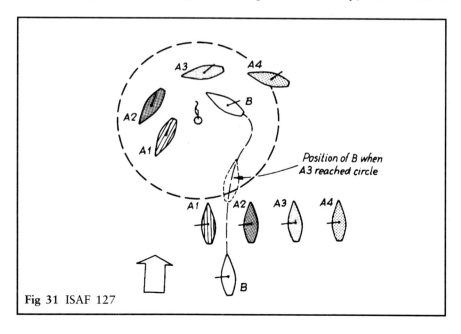

Position of B when A3 reached circle

Fig 31 ISAF 127

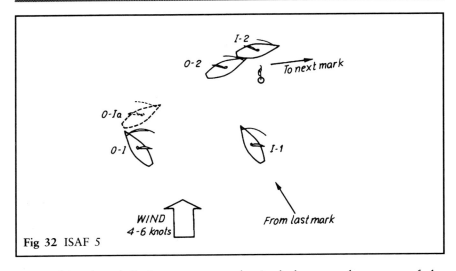

Fig 32 ISAF 5

on starboard and *Daisy* on port tack. And she must keep out of the way while *Daisy* passes the mark unless *Daisy* tacks; it makes no difference if *Daisy* gybes, or if *Buttercup* at that late stage obtains an overlap, *Buttercup* must still keep clear. But if *Daisy* tacks, then as soon as she passes through head to wind, rule 13 comes into force, and rule 18.2(b) no longer applies between them.

In ISAF 5 (Fig 32), O and I, both on port tack, reached towards a starboard-hand mark in a light wind. When O came abreast of the mark she was clear ahead of I, but three and a half lengths from the mark. I had reached the circle. O then gybed, headed for the mark and hit I on the transom. O protested I under rule 18.2(b); I protested O under rule 12. The protest committee disqualified O and she appealed.

Dismissing the appeal, the US Appeals Committee stated: 'O apparently believed that rule 18.2(b) applied when the two boats were at position 1 and that I, then being clear astern, was obliged to keep clear of O until both boats had passed the mark. As it states, rule 18.2(b) applies only if a boat is clear ahead when she reaches the two-length zone. At position 1, I was within two lengths of the mark, but O was well outside. When O gybed to sail to the mark the two became overlapped, and O was then obliged by rule 18.2(a) to give room to I to pass the mark, including room for her necessary gybe (although, in fact, after I's gybe she was clear ahead). To disqualify O for breaking rule 12 was proper since, in this situation, rule 18.2(b) did not modify rule 12.'

In ISAF 132 (Fig 33) the boats rounded the mark in a strong current, with a light wind. After rounding, A gybed on to port tack, set her

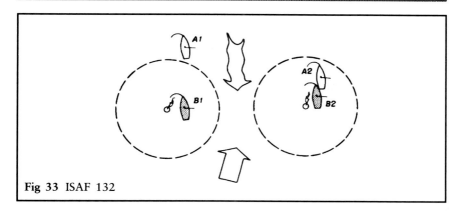

Fig 33 ISAF 132

spinnaker, and sailed downwind more than two lengths from the mark. B kept clear of A while A rounded, rounded herself, gybed and set her spinnaker, but the wind lightened and she did not clear the mark, the wind and current offsetting each other. As a result of the lightening wind and B's blanketing her, A began to drift backwards towards the mark and eventually there was minor contact.

A protested under rules 18.2(b) and 11, B protested under rule 18.2(a). The protest committee dismissed A's protest, upheld B's, and disqualified A for failing to give room to round the mark. A won her appeal: 'The boats were not overlapped as they approached the mark to round, and so B was required by rule 18.2(b) to keep clear of A until both boats had passed the mark. When contact occurred, B was not past the mark. Hence B was disqualified for breaking rule 18.2(b).'

Finally, look at RYA 69/6 (Fig 34). The clear-ahead boat could not claim the protection of rule 18.2(b) – she was too far ahead. W, having rounded the mark on to a starboard-tack run, met L beating up to the mark, also on starboard tack. In spite of W's attempts to maintain

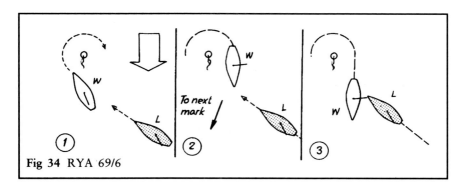

Fig 34 RYA 69/6

that she had right of way under rule 18.2(b), she was disqualified under rule 11. As is discussed under the definition Leeward and Windward, this is a particularly dangerous moment as the boats' closing speed is at a maximum.

Rule 18.2(c) The determining factor between rules 18.2(a) and (b) is the relative position of the two boats at the circle. You must think back to when you were last certain that you were overlapped, or not overlapped as the case may be. If you are not sure if the position has changed since that moment, then rule 18.2(c) requires everyone to presume that it has not. The inside boat claiming an overlap and the outside boat claiming to have broken an overlap, both take a risk. It is perhaps the most difficult point in the rule book for a jury to decide. If L is outside and her helmsman sits to windward he cannot see, while the would-be inside boat's helmsman – and crew usually – is in a bad position for judging an overlap. For these reasons, the rules here include their only onus clause (although the word 'onus' is not used because it is better to get away from the very complicated legal implications that that word bears in English law). Note that the rule is addressed to everybody: to both boats and to the protest committee. When the situation is in doubt, an outside boat must presume that the inside boat has an overlap; the inside boat must presume that the outside boat is clear ahead. The protest committee, having heard the evidence and still unable to decide, will presume that the last known position has remained unchanged.

It is most important to hear all the evidence; this is a 'last resort' rule and not to be lightly used as an easy way out of a protest hearing.

Rule 18.3 Tacking

Daisy (P) and *Buttercup* (S) arrive at the two-length circle of a windward mark on opposite tacks. *Daisy* tacks, completing her tack inside the circle and she must now watch her step. She may be overlapped, either as L, or W, or clear-ahead (if she is clear astern there is obviously no problem); but whatever her position, rule 18.2 does not apply. Look at Fig 35. In each case, *Daisy* has tacked (perhaps not always wisely) in the circle and is subject to rule 18.3. In position 1, she has got herself down to leeward; she may neither make W luff above close-hauled (so if W is on the layline, L will have to go the wrong side of the mark), nor, in any case, can she prevent W from rounding. In position 2, where again she has made herself L, rule 18.3(b) requires her to keep clear of an inside overlapped boat – in this case, W.

In position 3, if *Daisy* has tacked ahead and is now clear ahead and to weather, she is not in a strong position unless she is so far

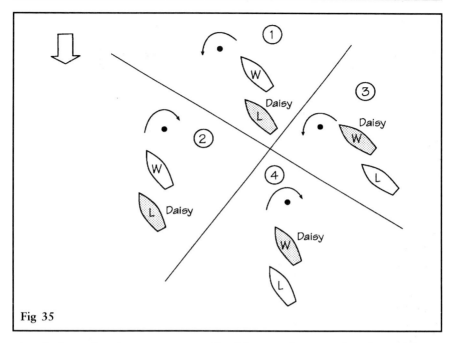

Fig 35

ahead that she does not cause L either to have to head up (above close-hauled) or to miss the mark by avoiding her. L has a right to sail straight on for the mark, and if she gets an overlap she becomes the right-of-way boat. Similarly, in position 3, if the overlap is established by the tack, W must keep clear of L. It is also specifically stated that, in these two situations, rule 15 (Acquiring Right of Way) does not apply, so L is given even more freedom than she normally has. In position 4, *Daisy*'s tack has made her inside boat to windward, so, since rule 18.2 is not active, she has no rights and must keep clear of L, and once again rule 15 does not apply.

Rule 18.4 Gybing

This is a rule addressed to the right-of-way boat, not to the boat being given room (where it is not necessary). It is addressed to an inside, overlapped boat with right of way whose proper course is to gybe, and it makes it clear that while she may sail her proper course round the mark, sail it she must, and she must gybe.

Note that if she does not have to gybe and is not subject to rule 17.1, she need not follow a proper course and can sail off into the blue.

In ISAF 151 (Fig 36), S did a tactical rounding, luffing 10–12 feet wide of the mark. When she bore away to gybe the boats touched. S

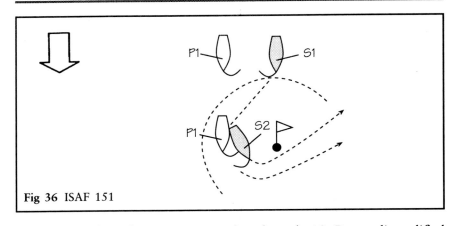

Fig 36 ISAF 151

protested under rule 10, P protested under rule 18. P was disqualified with the comment: 'The essential question is whether or not an inside starboard-tack boat may sail wide of the mark to make a tactically desirable rounding. There is no conflict here between rules 10 and 18; both apply and provide rights for the inside boat. The only limitation on the inside boat's starboard-tack rights is rule 18.4, which requires her to pass no farther from the mark than needed to sail her proper course. There is no question that S gybed in compliance with that rule.' P – arguing that since S luffed away from the mark and increased her distance from it, that was conclusive evidence she did not gybe as required by rule 18.4 – lost her appeal. The US Appeals Committee, agreeing with the protest committee, said: 'Until she gybed, rule 18.4 required S to sail no further from the mark than she had needed to sail her proper course, and the facts indicate that her course complied with that rule.'

Similarly, ISAF 166 states that when rules 18.2(a) and 18.4 apply at a leeward mark, an outside windward boat must keep sufficiently clear of the leeward boat that the leeward boat is able to sail her proper course while passing the mark.

Rule D1.1(b) alters rule 18.4 for team racing.

Rule 18.5 Passing a Continuing Obstruction
What is a continuing obstruction? A shore line, a river bank, a right-of-way boat are all examples of when rule 18.2 is modified. When *Buttercup* is overlapped inside *Daisy* as they run along the lake shore and when she drops back and becomes clear astern, *Daisy* can 'shut the door' and not allow *Buttercup* back in. On the other hand, *Buttercup*, if she sees a nice gap between *Daisy* and the shore, can come between them, when her obligations as clear-astern boat end.

There is nothing to stop *Buttercup* when she is L, and therefore right-of-way boat, from exercising her right to sail up to her proper course if that is not along the shore.

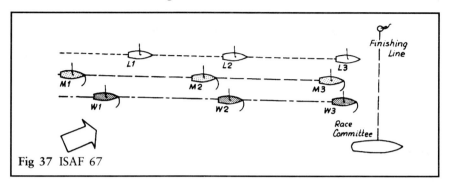

Fig 37 ISAF 67

ISAF 67 (Fig 37) shows three boats running for the finishing line; W and L were overlapped not quite two lengths apart when M sailed between them, and the three finished with no narrowing of space between L and W and no contact. W protested M for taking room to which she was not entitled, citing rule 18.2(b). The protest was dismissed on the grounds that L and W had left enough room for M to intervene safely. Dismissing W's appeal, the RYA stated: 'Under the definition, L was an obstruction to W, as she was to M as well, because they were both required to keep clear of her. Was she a continuing obstruction? Once W overhauled L, the two boats sailed overlapped at least six lengths towards the finishing line. That was easily long enough to qualify L as a continuing obstruction. Since M was able to intervene safely, which she demonstrated by performance, she broke no rule.'

In ISAF 76 (Fig 38), where boats are racing among breakwaters, questions were asked about their status. When the boats tack at position 2 they are more than two lengths from the end of the breakwater. BW, outside, is required by rule 18.2(a) to give room to AL, inside room to pass the obstruction. While the breakwater is a continuous structure from the shore to its outer end, it is not a continuing obstruction within the meaning of the rule, since the boats are concerned only with the very end.

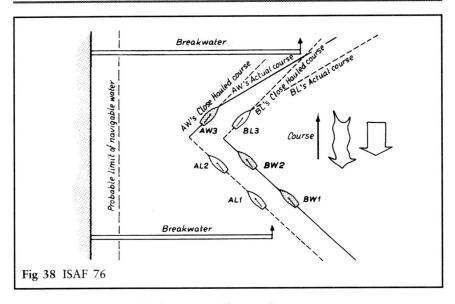

Fig 38 ISAF 76

Rule 19 Room to Tack at an Obstruction

19.1 When safety requires a close-hauled boat to make a substantial course change to avoid an *obstruction* and she intends to tack, but cannot tack and avoid another boat on the same *tack*, she shall hail for *room* to do so. Before tacking she shall give the hailed boat time to respond. The hailed boat shall either

   (a) tack as soon as possible, in which case the hailing boat shall also tack as soon as possible, or

   (b) immediately reply 'You tack', in which case the hailing boat shall immediately tack and the hailed boat shall give *room*, and rules 10 and 13 do not apply.

19.2 Rule 19.1 does not apply at a starting *mark* or its anchor line surrounded by navigable water from the time boats are approaching them to *start* until they have passed them or at a *mark* that the hailed boat can fetch. When rule 19.1 applies, rule 18 does not.

This is a safety rule that permits a close-hauled boat, caught between another on the same tack and the shore, to avoid them both without substantial loss of distance. (The rule does not exist in IRPCS, so be careful when they are in force; the boat to weather of you does not have to tack off if you hail, although she may do so in the interests of safety – and then she may well protest.)

In what follows, the boats are called L and W, but while the hailing boat may be the leeward boat, they need not be overlapped and the hailing boat may be clear ahead but down to leeward. (Strictly speaking, according to the definition, the terms *windward* and *leeward* apply only when boats are overlapped.)

L, beating up the coast, knows she is getting near the rocks; she knows too that she cannot tack without hitting W. She hails for room to tack; in the UK, the hail is 'room' or 'water', in France 'eau', in Italy 'aqua'; it does not matter that the language is different – the need is made clear by the urgency. Standing on the shore as boats come past, the cries can be heard from far away. Now W must act and she has a choice. She can either tack or she can shout back, 'You tack', and in either case L will tack and W (now P or S) will make it possible for L to avoid a collision. Most problems arise on a left-hand shore because when L tacks she finds W on starboard. Now LP must either pass ahead of WS, and WS will bear away if necessary, or LP must pass astern of S and there must be room for her to do so, even though she may have to bear away. Let us look at how this works.

The boats must be on the same tack; ISAF 93 (Fig 25), which we looked at under rule 10, shows what happens when they are not, as does RYA 84/11.

The manoeuvre must be necessitated by danger; US 116 (Fig 39) shows PL calling for room to tack from PW to avoid the obstruction formed by S. PW failed to tack and S had to tack back on to port to avoid a collision. S protested PL and PW under rule 10, and PL protested PW under rule 19.1. PW was disqualified and PL exonerated.

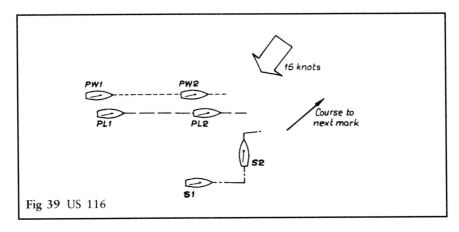

Fig 39 US 116

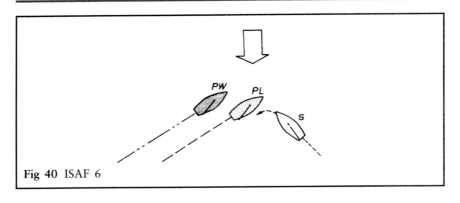

Fig 40 ISAF 6

Very similarly, in ISAF 6 (Fig 40), S hailed PL, and PL in turn twice hailed for room to tack. PW did not respond and S, now very close to PL, had to bear away smartly to avoid her. PW retired and S protested PL under rule 10. The protest committee disqualified PL, but on appeal she was reinstated. 'Having hailed three times, PL was entitled to expect that PW would respond and give her room to tack. She was not obliged either to anticipate PW's failure to comply with rule 19.1 or to bear away astern of the S, the obstruction.'

US 81 is another good example of how the rule works. L must believe that if she tacks she will collide, and if W is misled by a hail and responds by tacking, she can protest L.

L must hail – 'she shall hail' – but what happens if the hail is not heard? In ISAF 117, L hailed, waited a moment or so, got no response, tacked, bore away and collided with W. W, it turned out, had not heard the hail. The US Appeals Committee, upholding W's appeal against her disqualification, stated: 'The failure of a hailed boat to hear an adequate hail would not necessarily relieve her of her obligations under rule 19 to a leeward boat. Where, however, as in this case, the leeward boat observed no response after her hail, a second and more vigorous hail would be required to constitute proper notice of her intention to tack.'

When you must tack, hail in good time and hail as loud as you can.

L must not tack as she hails; she must give W time to respond. In US 131, L hailed loudly for room to tack and put her helm down immediately. W protested L for infringing rule 19.1 for hailing and tacking simultaneously, and L was disqualified. Confirming this decision, the US Appeals Committee said, 'it was L's duty first to hail and then to tack.'

As we said, W can either tack herself as soon as possible, or she can hail in her turn 'you tack'. L hails for 'room to tack', and the definition Room means that this is the space a boat needs, while manoeuvring promptly in a seamanlike way. It does not mean that W, when she replies 'you tack', must keep clear; she need only give room. On a left-hand shore, if after L has tacked and become P she finds that she must bear away to avoid W, now S, then she must do so. However, if her manoeuvre had to be 'unseamanlike', S might still be protested successfully. ISAF 80 (Fig 41) illustrates this. As the two boats neared the shore, L hailed W for room whereupon W replied: 'Take my stern'. L interpreted that to mean 'you tack', and tacked immediately. After tacking she had to bear away to pass under W's stern which she cleared by 3 feet. She protested W under rule 19.1. The protest committee decided that W had not given enough room and disqualified her. She appealed, and the decision was reversed. 'L, the tacking boat (now P) demonstrated by her actions that she had room to tack and clear W (now S). Therefore rule 19.1 did not apply. Neither boat broke a rule.' US 11 is a similar case except that, after PW had failed to respond (and she was disqualified under rule 19.1), PL still had the possibility of bearing away astern of S which she did not do. It was held that she should have done so and she was disqualified under rule 10. The fact that PW broke a rule did not, in the circumstances, relieve PL of her obligations to S.

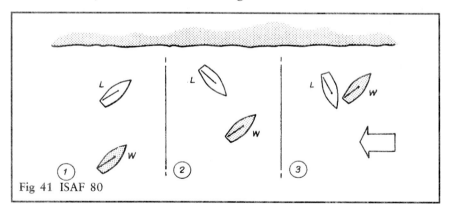

Fig 41 ISAF 80

RYA 73/5 (Fig 42) states that one of the objects of the rule is to ensure that both boats tack as nearly as possible at the same time. As can be seen in Fig 42, L carried on and did not tack 'as soon as possible'. RYA 82/6 (Fig 43) shows us L luffing so slowly that she delayed the completion of her tack beyond a reasonable time and thus was disqualified.

Let us finally look at what usually happens: *Daisy*, close-hauled, sees she is nearing the shore and realizes that she will not be able to

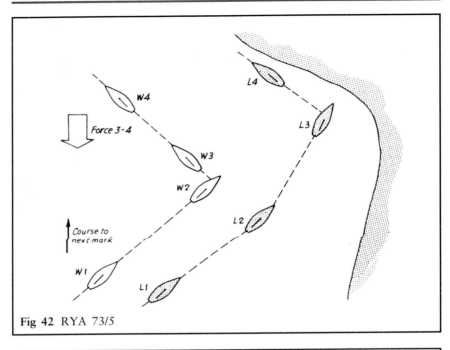

Fig 42 RYA 73/5

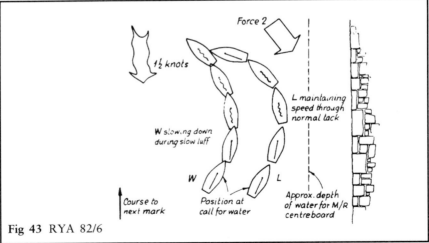

Fig 43 RYA 82/6

clear W on her starboard quarter if she tacks. Some distance off (depending on the weather, the type of shore, her draft, etc), she loudly hails 'water' (perhaps 'shore room' in the USA), her helmsman probably turning so that his voice carries. W, who has been expecting the call, almost immediately tacks (as soon as she can let fly her genoa), and within a second or two *Daisy* tacks too, certain now that there will be no collision. Because *Daisy* has to be given room she is an obstruction, and when she is the leeward of several boats, they must all tack to give room (if necessary). To hear the hails and to see a number of boats all tack, virtually at once, is almost like watching a ballet. It is one of the most commonly used rules, and over the years has been extremely successful in avoiding accidents.

Rule 19.2 brings, as usual, two exceptions:

1 As boats come up to the committee vessel, or – if it is big enough to be an obstruction – to the pin end to start, they have no rights under rule 19.1. L, if she hails for room, either will not get it or, if she tacks, will be protested for infringing rule 13. The windward or the clear-astern boat is under no obligation to give room for a tack, and can in theory drive L on to the committee boat, so *beware*! This rule was only adopted, some years ago, after long discussion; it was considered more dangerous for L to be allowed to hail for room and tack into a long line of boats than to take the other options open to her (go to the other side of the committee boat or let her sheets go and drop back, for example).

2 When L and W are going for an obstruction that is also a mark and L cannot fetch but W can, L may not call for water to tack.

Section D – Other Rules

> *When rule 20 or 21 applies between two boats, Section A rules do not.*

Preamble
Note that rules 10, 11, 12 and 13 do not apply between two boats affected by rule 20 or rule 21.This does not apply to rule 22.

Rule 20 Starting Errors; Penalty Turns; Moving Astern

> A boat sailing towards the pre-start side of the starting line or its extensions to comply with rule 29.1 or rule 30.1 shall *keep clear* of a boat not doing so until she is completely on the pre-start side. A boat making penalty turns shall *keep clear* of one that is not. A boat moving astern by backing a sail shall *keep clear* of one that is not.

1 Starting Errors, applying to rules 29.1 and 30.1   Rule 29.1 requires *Daisy*, when she has been over the line at the start, to return and start correctly. While she is returning she must keep clear of all the other boats that have started correctly and are on their way to the first mark. This means that her trip back may be long and difficult.

Rule 30.1 (I Flag Rule). When, during the minute before the starting signal, *Daisy* is over the line and is making her way back to start, she has no rights save those arising from rules 14 and 16.

2 Penalty Turns   *Daisy* loses any rights she might have under rules 10, 11, 12 and 13 and is only protected by rules 14 and 16 and, in this case, by rule 22.2.

3 Moving Astern   Other than for sailboards, this is a new rule, and it will be interesting to see how it works out. *Daisy*'s backward movement must be through the water (the tide carrying her backwards past the anchored committee boat doesn't count) and she must sail backwards because she is backing a sail. Thus she is unlikely to lose her rights by mistake, only if she does so deliberately (usually to avoid going over the starting line early) will she get into trouble.

Rule C2.4 alters rule 20 with respect to taking a penalty.

Rule 21 Capsized, Anchored or Aground; Rescuing

> If possible, a boat shall avoid a boat that is capsized or has not regained control after capsizing, is anchored or aground, or is trying to help a person or vessel in danger. A boat is capsized when her masthead is in the water.

Suddenly, *Buttercup* capsizes or runs aground in front of *Daisy*; rules 10, 11, 12 and 13 cease to apply between them, and *Daisy* must do her very best to avoid a collision. At the same time, her relationships with a third boat remain as usual and, since *Buttercup* has broken no rule, *Daisy* cannot be exonerated for breaking (say) rule 10 and hitting the third boat. However, I trust that in real life, there being no [old] 'rule 33' to worry about, no protest would be forthcoming from a genuine unavoidable accident of this sort.

Note there is a positive statement that a boat that has her masthead in the water is capsized. There is no statement that a boat that has not got her masthead in the water is not capsized.

Daisy must also avoid a boat anchored or going to help another in distress, but in these cases there would probably be a bit more time.

Rule 22 Interfering with Another Boat

22.1 If reasonably possible, a boat not *racing* shall not interfere with a boat that is *racing*.

22.2 A boat shall not deliberately interfere with a boat making penalty turns to delay her.

It would be unfair if a boat that had finished and was no longer racing could sail back and, if not sink, at least hinder, or interfere with, one still trying to finish. It is also necessary to make boats that are no longer racing keep a good look-out; they are getting sails down, perhaps celebrating a win, and it is easy to forget the others.

RYA 96/1 looked at an odd set of circumstances. One class was racing through the starting line of another just at the moment a general recall was signalled. As a result, S, in the second class, was suddenly not racing. S tried to keep clear of port-tack boats coming through the line; she missed two but hit the third. P was disqualified for infringing rule 10 and appealed. Dismissing her appeal, the RYA said that the rules of Part 2 applied to all boats, because they were racing or had been racing, and that rule 22.1 did not require a boat not racing to keep clear. It followed that P's obligation under rule 10 was in force: she was the give-way boat and was required to keep clear. This she failed to do. S, trying to fulfil her obligation under rule 22.1, bore away to go astern of P, which resulted in her infringing rule 16 and colliding with another boat. This was due to P's breach of rule 10 and S was exonerated under rule 64.1(b).

It is unfair to harry a boat that is doing her penalty turns. How 'interfering' is to be interpreted remains to be seen.

Rule C2.6 alters rule 22 for match racing; rule D1.1(c) alters rule 22 for team racing.

(Numbers 23 and 24 are spare numbers)

Part 3 – Conduct of a Race

Rule 25 Sailing Instructions and Signals

> Sailing instructions shall be made available to each boat before a race begins. The race committee shall conduct the race using the visual and sound signals defined in the Race Signals and any other signals included in the sailing instructions.

It is obviously no good writing sailing instructions if they do not reach the competitors. For club races, the notice board may be adequate, but for more important events each boat should receive a copy. The rule applies just as much to changes as it does to the original sailing instructions; it is no good making a necessary, sensible change if the boats never get to hear of it. See rule 88.2 for further details.

The flag and sound signals illustrated in Race Signals are governed by this rule, and will be used by the race committee unless sailing instructions alter any or some of the meanings (quoting rule 25), the meaning of each will be as printed. There are no grounds for redress when these signals are not seen, or not understood, by competitors; this was made clear in RYA 82/17: 'Although the race committee's decision to abandon the race was improper, the fact remains that its signal was made in accordance with rule 25 and most of the competitors complied with it. There is no rule that requires a race committee to ensure that every yacht receives its signals.' In US 170 it was held: 'A flag is "displayed" within the meaning of the Race Signals and constitutes proper notice under rules 27 and 32 when it is hoisted or otherwise placed in a position customarily used for signalling purposes and in which the flag reasonably could be expected by the competitors. That the flag hangs limp because of lack of wind does not alter the fact that it is "displayed".' When there is no wind, you may have a problem!

Just as fleet signals between ships used to be accompanied by a gun, each flag has its sound signal; a helmsman cannot keep his eyes fixed on the committee boat, so his attention must be drawn to the display of a visual signal by a noise. Any loud noise will do: a hooter, a whistle or a gun – but, unless specified in sailing instructions, *not* a voice (RYA 77/1). There must be some reasonable possibility of the sound being heard within the necessary distance on an average day. A small hooter will suffice for a short starting line, but only a cannon will carry across a line suitable for 100 offshore racers. It is particularly important for a repetitive sound signal denoting a change of course or a mark missing (flags C and M) to be clearly audible over wind and water and sounded before boats get engrossed in mark rounding.

When possible, a recall gun signal should be of the same strength as the starting gun.

There is one problem, ISAF 70 states that if a visual signal is not accompanied by the required sound signal, a boat that has been prejudiced may get redress, but rule 26.1 says that the failure of a sound signal shall be disregarded. I take it that the rule, which would override an interpretation, refers solely to starting signals, the timing of which every helmsman has on his watch, but not to other signals such as the individual recall signal. ISAF 134 confirms this, underlining the absolute necessity for a sound signal with the recall signal.

The race committee must not only follow the signals in the rule book, but it must also score according to the rule book (Appendix A), unless in either case sailing instructions tell it to do something else. Scoring details are discussed in the text on Appendix A, but I shall say here what I shall repeat later: that scoring is of vital importance. The racing can be wonderful, the weather perfect, the parties super, but if the scoring system is ambiguous so that two people think they should have won at the end, they will go away unhappy. Always check it very carefully before racing starts to make sure there are no nasty surprises.

Rule 26 Starting Systems 1 and 2

26.1 A race shall be started by using either System 1 or System 2. Signals shall be made at five-minute intervals. Times shall be taken from the visual signals; the failure of a sound signal shall be disregarded. Signals shall be as follows (flags of a single colour may be replaced by shapes of the same colour):

Signal	System 1	System 2
Warning	Class flag; 1 sound	Yellow flag; 1 sound
Preparatory	Flag P; 1 sound	Blue flag; 1 sound
Starting	Flags removed; 1 sound	Red flag; 1 sound

26.2 In System 1, when classes are started at ten-minute intervals, the warning signal for each succeeding class shall be displayed at the starting signal of the preceding class. When five-minute intervals are used, flag P shall be left displayed until the last class starts and the warning signal for each succeeding class shall be displayed at the time of the preparatory signal of the preceding class. If there is a general recall, the warning and preparatory signals of any succeeding classes shall be removed immediately after the general recall has been signalled.

26.3 In System 2, each signal shall be removed one minute before the next is made. When classes are started at ten-minute intervals, the starting signal for each class shall be the warning signal for the next. When classes are started at five-minute intervals, the preparatory signal for each class shall be the warning signal for the next. When class flags are used, they shall be displayed before or with the preparatory signal for the class.

Race committees can use any starting system they like, but the two systems described in this rule (System 1 mostly used in North America and System 2 in Europe) are well and truly tried. There is a third system in Appendix N, 11.1. Since Appendix N is not published in this book, here is the sailing instruction: 'N11.1 Races will be started using System 3. This changes rule 26.1. Times shall be taken from the visual signals; the failure of a sound signal shall be disregarded. Signals will be as follows:

Title	Signals
Warning	Class flag, 1 sound
Preparatory	Flag P, Z, I, blue or black flag; 1 sound
Starting	Flags removed, 1 sound

The preparatory signal will be displayed one minute after the warning signal and will be removed, with one sound, one minute before the starting signal. The starting signal will be displayed five minutes after the preparatory signal.'

Race officers are being encouraged to try this new system; it will shorten the gillying about at the start and need one less halyard – two benefits worth considering.

Times are taken from the visual signals, while the mistiming or failure of a sound signal may be disregarded, but this refers only to starting sound signals (see under rule 25). Errors in starting sequences are common, either because of mistiming or incorrect signals. Whenever possible, a race committee aware of the error should postpone (before the starting signal) or abandon (after) and restart the sequence. When this is not done, the start is valid until one or more yachts can show that their finishing positions were significantly prejudiced; it is then that redress must be considered – nearly always a very unsatisfactory procedure.

Rule 27 Other Race Committee Actions Before the Starting Signal

27.1 No later than the warning signal, the race committee shall signal or otherwise designate the course to be sailed if the sailing instructions have not stated the course, and it may replace one course signal with another, signal that a designated short course will be used (flag S), and apply rule 40 (flag Y).

27.2 No later than the preparatory signal, the race committee may move a starting *mark* and may apply rule 30.

27.3 Before the starting signal, the race committee may *postpone* (flag AP) or *abandon* the race (flag N over H or A) for any reason.

Rule 27.1 Before the Warning Signal
Sometimes a flag or numeral pennant shows which of a number of courses is to be used, and sometimes a courseboard lists the marks to be rounded, or they are broadcast by radio. Whatever the method, the course must be communicated to the competitors before the warning signal. When that is impossible, the race must be postponed until the course can be displayed correctly when a new starting sequence can begin. In RYA 87/4, the race committee tried to alter rule 27.1 so as to be able to announce the course between the warning and preparatory signals, but failed to make specific reference to the change as required by rule 86.2, so the sailing instruction was invalid. In addition, the course was in fact announced after the preparatory signal. No wonder the boat got redress! The race committee may change the course too; for example, having set course A, it can, before the warning signal, change that to course B, or to a previously designated shortened course, and it must then also apply rule 40, flag Y, if it wants lifejackets to be worn.

Rule 27.2 Before the Preparatory Signal
1 The starting line may be fixed. Any starting mark can be relaid (after the 'prep' a postponement will be necessary). This is a recurrent problem for race committees in shifting winds and strong tides. If a committee boat, used as a starting mark, is to be held on her engines and not anchored, this fact is better mentioned in sailing instructions.

2 Flag I, flag Z or the black flag may be hoisted, indicating special starting penalties (see rule 30).

Rule 27.3 Before the Start

If something happens just before the start, a race committee may be understandably unwilling to abort and start the whole procedure over again, but, although it is tough on those who were about to make the perfect start (and what a lot there are!), it is the road that leads to endless unsatisfactory redress hearings. Postpone, abandon (see rule 32), signal a general recall (see rule 29.3), but do not let the race go.

A postponement or abandonment may be made at any time up to the starting signal and for any reason. This presumably includes waiting for boats that are coming out late for the start. This practice often infuriates those who have arrived on time, but it seems within the competence of the race officer. However, I believe the 'reason' must be 'proper' (see rule 62, Redress). For example, a race officer who made the fleet wait for his son, or for a boat of his own nation in a big international championship, – without some *very* good excuse – might open the way for redress.

Rule 28 Sailing the Course

28.1 A boat shall *start*, pass each *mark* on the required side in the correct order, and *finish*, so that a string representing her wake after *starting* and until *finishing* would, when drawn taut, lie on the required side of each *mark* and touch each rounding *mark*. She may correct any errors to comply with this rule, provided she has not already *finished*. After *finishing*, a boat need not cross the finishing line completely.

28.2 A *mark* has a required side for a boat only when she is on a leg that the *mark* begins, bounds or ends, except that a starting *mark* begins to have a required side when she is approaching the starting line from its pre-start side to *start*.

All rules are equal, but if some are more important than others, then rule 28 is one of the most important in the book, for it is the rule that compels competitors to sail the correct course if they wish to get into the results. Let us look at it in detail.

Daisy must first start correctly in accordance with the definition Start. This is so easy to say, but so difficult to do at the right moment, with over-enthusiasm leading to individual and general recalls, new starts, redress, etc.

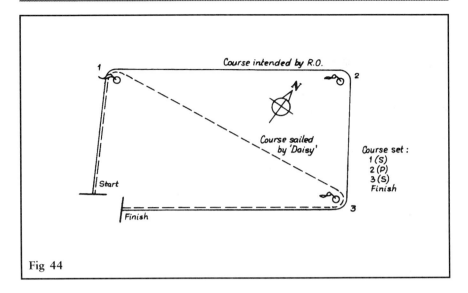

Fig 44

Then she must pass each mark on the required side in the correct order. Rule M2.1(4) requires sailing instructions to describe the course in a comprehensible way, a surprisingly difficult job. Rule 28 obliges *Daisy* to follow this course and supplies a method for checking that she has done so. The piece of string rule is an aid to setting courses and to deciding whether they have been sailed correctly. Looking at Fig 44, we see that *Daisy* sailed the course that was posted, although it was not that intended by the course setter. If she was really meant to round mark 2 there are three ways of getting her to do so: require boats to pass to the north of mark 2 (rarely used); require the mark to be *rounded*, in which case the string must touch it, and the mark will have to be looped by sailing 270° round it (usually undesirable); or, more easily, require it to be left to starboard instead of to port. Since the race committee did none of these things, *Daisy* could not be disqualified for failing to sail the course. Naturally, we can all guess that the race officer had mistakenly put P when he meant S, but courses cannot be set by telepathy.

The words 'touch each rounding mark' stop clever corner-cutting when there is no doubt that the mark is a rounding (or turning) mark. Such a mark has aptly been described as one that *lengthens* the course, and it is thus important to specify which marks are to be rounded. US 275 arose from a disaster caused by a mark being posted as P instead of S and it was said: 'The sailing instructions should differentiate boundary marks from rounding marks: when they fail to do so they are ambiguous, boats sailing any course which conforms to the posted one should not be penalized.' RYA 86/4 underlines the importance of distinguishing between rounding and boundary marks; describing the course, it states that an instruction that a mark is to be passed does not establish its status as a rounding mark.

Finally, *Daisy* must finish according to the definition Finish. When the race committee tries to alter this by putting in a hook finish and *Daisy* obeys the race committee rather than the definition, she will not have finished and should be scored DNF.

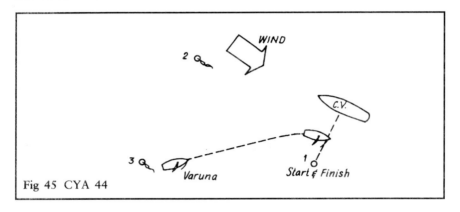

Fig 45 CYA 44

In CYA 44 (Fig 45), the course set was 'Twice round the triangle 1, 2, 3, leaving all marks to port.' *Varuna* crossed the finishing line 'in the direction of the course from the last mark [no. 3]'. Other boats crossed the line in the other direction having rounded mark 1 – now a finishing mark – to port. The race committee scored *Varuna* and other boats that had sailed a similar course DNF, but on appeal this was reversed, and they were reinstated. Presumably those boats that finished contrary to the definition were then marked DNF. Had the committee boat moved after the start to the other side of the mark, boats finishing correctly would have left mark 1 to port and thus avoided the rather telling, though fruitless, argument that *Varuna* did not complete the course because she did not complete two rounds leaving all marks to port as specified. Other cases and decisions, including ISAF 102 (Fig 54), confirm this case.

These 'hook' finishes happen with depressing regularity, most frequently as a result of shortening course. They arise in part from a misunderstanding of the way the nature of a mark can change. In Fig 45, mark 1 serves as a starting mark, a rounding mark (at the end of the first round) and as a finishing mark. Its required side is decided

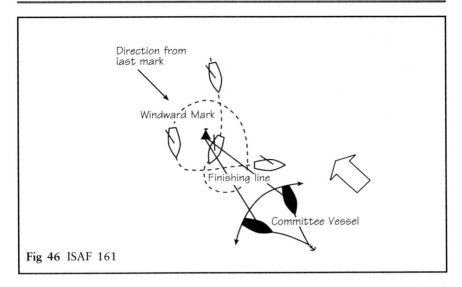

Fig 46 ISAF 161

in the first and third instances *by facts on the water* in accordance with the definitions of starting and finishing; only for the second – the rounding marks – is it possible to select the required side by means of sailing instructions.

It can happen that the finishing line lies in the same direction as the course from the last mark. What then? ISAF 161 (Fig 46) shows the end of a race where *White Satin* crossed the line in the direction, as she believed, from the last mark, logging her finishing time. Hearing no sound signal, she returned across the line when the race officer timed her and gave her a signal. The committee boat was swinging either side of the leeward/windward line while the race officer watched closely, finishing only those boats he believed were finishing correctly. On appeal, *White Satin* was given her first finishing time. 'When a boat,' said the RYA, 'cannot reasonably ascertain in which direction she should finish so as to conform to the definition, she is entitled to finish in either direction. Finishing lines should be laid as nearly as possible at right angles to the direction of the last leg of the course. It is highly undesirable that the line should be laid so that it lies in a direct line.' This case must be clearly distinguished from CYA 44 discussed earlier.

And the way we can check all this? Tie a piece of string to the boat's stern and, when she has finished, pull it tight. It must cross the starting line, leave every mark on the correct side, being hard up against any marks described in the sailing instructions as rounding marks, or marks that are to be rounded, and reach the finishing line.

Further problems with starting and finishing are discussed under their own definitions.

When *Daisy* thinks she has passed a mark on the wrong side she may, provided she has not finished, unwind and sail the correct course. The string will, of course, when tight, come on the right side.

It is important to note that there is no racing rule that exempts a boat that has been forced the wrong side of a mark from sailing the course, nor is redress available (RYA 82/10).

RYA cases 66/11 and 88/9 also deal with these problems.

Rule 28.2 A mark is an object that sailing instructions require a boat to pass on a specified side (see definition Mark), and sailing instructions must describe the marks and state the order and side on which each is to be left (see rule M2.1(4)). Rule 28 states that boats must pass marks on their required side, but now we are told *when* marks have a required side. There are three main categories of marks: starting marks, finishing marks, and course marks. Course marks may be rounding or boundary marks; you pass a rounding mark just as you pass a boundary mark.

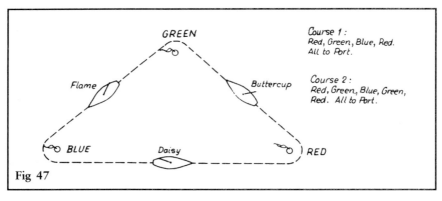

Fig 47

1   A course mark has a required side only for a boat that is on a leg that it begins, bounds or ends. Looking at Fig 47, Course 1: Green is a mark for *Buttercup* because Green ends the leg from Red to Green; Green is a mark for *Flame* because it begins the leg from Green to Blue; Green is not a mark for *Daisy* because she is on the leg from Blue to Red and she may pass either side of Green (which she might wish to do on a beat) and would not infringe rule 31 by touching it.

If Course 2 is set, the boats in fact sail the same course as Course 1, but Green is a boundary mark for *Daisy* on her leg from Blue to Red; she may neither touch Green nor leave it to starboard with impunity. In fact, Course 2 might be clearer if it were written 'Red, Green, Blue, Red, all marks to be rounded to port. When on the leg from Blue to Red, boats shall not pass north of Green' or similar.

It is important to remember that in the same race the same buoy can, and often does, serve as starting, rounding and finishing mark. It must be considered according to its status at any given moment.

2 A starting mark is 'untouchable' after the preparatory signal when racing begins (rule 31.1), but *Daisy* may pass any side of it until she approaches it to start, when the required side may be deduced from the definition Start. It may also be stated in the sailing instructions, but if (improbably) the two contradict each other, the definition will prevail. The required side of the starting limit marks must be specified in the sailing instructions.

When the starting line is a transit, the distance mark may be on the course side of the starting line. It acquires a required side as the boats near the line to start and no difficulties arise, but when it is laid on or has drifted to the pre-start side of the line, the object of the mark, to limit the end of the line, may be defeated. Over the last 50 years a number of cases have held that when the mark is more than one boat length from the line, on the pre-start side, it has no required side and can be ignored. This is discussed under 'Mark'. The situation is unsatisfactory, but not for want of efforts to right it; it is an intractable problem (RYA 65/18 refers).

ISAF 124 deals with the situation at the end of a race when a finishing limit mark is on the post-finish side of the line and can be ignored.

Generally speaking, if you are setting a course, or are going to sail it, draw it out roughly on paper to make sure all is clear.

Rule 29 Starting; Recalls

29.1 On the Course Side at the Start
When at her starting signal any part of a boat's hull, crew or equipment is on the course side of the starting line, the boat shall sail completely to the pre-start side of the line before *starting*.

29.2 Individual Recall
When at her starting signal a boat must comply with rule 29.1 or rule 30.1, the race committee shall promptly display flag X. The signal shall be displayed until all such boats are completely on the pre-start side of the starting line or its extensions and have complied with rule 30.1 if it applies, but not later than four minutes after the starting signal or one minute before any later starting signal, whichever is earlier.

> **29.3 General Recall**
>
> When at the starting signal several unidentified boats are on the course side of the starting line or there has been an error in the starting procedure, the race committee may signal a general recall (flag First Substitute). The preparatory signal for a new start for the recalled class shall be made one minute after the First Substitute is lowered, and the starts for any succeeding classes shall follow the new start.

Rule 29.1 On the Course Side at the Start

Rule 29.1 requires a boat to start in accordance with the definition. This rule states unequivocally that in order to start correctly, a boat must first be entirely on the pre-start side of the line. It is always a sad sight to see a boat that was over the line coming back, turning round, and then sailing off before she has completely recrossed the line. It is also the source of many unsuccessful claims for redress. The phrase 'on the course side of the starting line' is used because it covers both situations envisaged by the rule: that of the boat coming to the line from the pre-start side and pushing two inches of her bow over just before the gun goes, and that of the boat on the course side of the line which has arrived late and never reached the pre-start side.

Note that in those rare races where the organizers want to penalize early starters instead of recalling them, it is permissible to alter rules 28.1 and 29 to achieve this end. But it should only be used in very special circumstances, like the start of the Whitbread Round the World Race where the crowded waters at the start make it impracticable to return in order to start correctly.

Rule 29.2 Individual Recall

When a boat is over the line at the start every effort must be made to tell her, and to tell her quickly, so that she can correct her mistake without losing too much. Every experienced sailor and race officer will know how difficult it is to achieve accurate, intelligible, speedy recall signals. The rule uses flag X, and any other common method (such as leaving the class flag at the dip) must be prescribed by the sailing instructions. It has been held that a hail is insufficient for the sound signal, so prescribe that too if required.

If the race committee makes a mistake in whichever system has been chosen, *Daisy* may ask for redress if her finishing position has been prejudiced (see rule 62.1(a)).

ISAF 157, where the recall signal was given 40 seconds after the starting signal, states that redress may be obtained by those boats scored OCS, and discusses at length the sort of redress that might be suitable.

In RYA 67/3, the race officer made a mistake and lowered the class flag before one boat had recrossed the line. Seeing this she sailed off and was scored DNS. Redress was refused by the protest committee, which said that the race officer's mistake did not relieve the boat of her duty to return properly. On appeal, the RYA disagreed: 'the race committee cannot escape its obligations by placing the responsibility in the boat concerned'.

If, however, a boat is aware that she was over the line at the start, does not return across it and does not retire, she is cheating. She is acting against the fundamental principle in 'Sportsmanship and the Rules' and breaks rule 2.

It is not enough to make the visual signal without the sound signal; in such a case, an early starter, when in doubt, is not required to respond to a recall (ISAF 70).

Rule 29.3 General Recall

A general recall is signalled (First Substitute) when there are a number of *unidentified* premature starters or when the race committee makes a mistake. When the race officer can identify all the boats that are over, he is not justified in recalling the whole fleet. This was illustrated long ago when, in a fleet of forty-odd, all except three boats started early. No one returned and, much to their indignation, all except the three were disqualified. There was no redress and an appeal failed.

Unless sailing instructions say something different, the starting sequence begins again at the preparatory signal one minute after the First Substitute is lowered, giving the fleet just five minutes to resettle itself.

Boats have often infringed rules before the general recall signal, but they cannot be penalized for any such misdeeds except for any under rule 69 (see rule 36). This does not mean that an incident must be disregarded altogether. If *Daisy* is damaged in an incident with *Buttercup* and then there is a general recall, *Buttercup* cannot be penalized but *Daisy* can protest her, and if *Buttercup* is found to have infringed a rule, *Daisy* can get redress under rule 62.1(a).

Between the recall signal and the new preparatory signal, the boats are not racing, so, under rule 22.1, they must not, if possible, interfere with boats in other classes that are racing. RYA 96/1 covers this point and is discussed under that rule.

Rule 30 Starting Penalties

30.1 I Flag Rule

If flag I has been displayed before or with her preparatory signal, and any part of a boat's hull, crew or equipment is on the course side of the starting line or its extensions during the minute before her starting signal, she shall sail to the pre-start side of the line around either end before *starting*.

30.2 Z Flag Rule

If flag Z has been displayed before or with her preparatory signal, and any part of a boat's hull, crew or equipment is identified within the triangle formed by the ends of the starting line and the first *mark* during the minute before her starting signal and a general recall is then signalled, she shall, without a hearing, be given a 20% scoring penalty calculated as stated in rule 44.3(c). If the race is restarted, resailed or rescheduled, she shall still be given the penalty.

30.3 Black Flag Rule

If a black flag has been displayed before or with her preparatory signal, and any part of a boat's hull, crew or equipment is identified within the triangle formed by the ends of the starting line and the first *mark* during the minute before her starting signal, the boat will be disqualified without a hearing. If the race is restarted, resailed or rescheduled, she is not entitled to compete in it. If a general recall is signalled or the race is *abandoned*, the race committee shall display her sail number.

When a large number of starters makes race control difficult, there are several special starting systems of various grades of severity that the race officer can use, and he can use each at the hoisting of a flag. This is fine for experienced race officers controlling big fleets, but others with small fleets, should avoid using them unless essential. Note that none of the three starting systems, I flag, Z flag, or black flag, operate until there is a starting signal; a nippy race officer who manages to postpone, even two seconds before the starting gun, can start again with a clean sheet.

Rule 30.1 I Flag Rule

When *Daisy* is on the course side of the line at any time after one minute to the starting signal, she may not, as is usual, dip back across the line, but instead must go round the end of it (the committee boat or the ODM) across one if its extensions before she can start correctly.

Rule 30.2 Z Flag Rule

This is a relatively new, untried system, but is said to be preferable to the I flag rule. If *Daisy* is over the line and there is no general recall, she will have a normal individual recall and can either return and start correctly, or be scored OCS at the end of the race. Only after a general recall will she be penalized.

Rule 30.3 Black Flag Rule

Responding to popular demand, this drastic starting system is now out of the sailing instruction guide and into the rule book. The move will ensure consistency of wording, but it is to be hoped that the system will be used only for large fleets and as rarely as possible.

Rule 31 Touching a Mark

31.1 While *racing*, a boat shall not touch a starting *mark* before *starting*, a *mark* that begins, bounds or ends the leg of the course on which she is sailing, or a finishing *mark* after *finishing*.

31.2 A boat that has broken rule 31.1 may, after getting well clear of other boats as soon as possible, take a penalty by promptly making one complete 360° turn including one tack and one gybe. When a boat takes the penalty after touching a finishing *mark*, she shall return completely to the course side of the line before *finishing*. However, if a boat has gained a significant advantage in the race or series by touching the *mark*, she shall retire.

31.3 When a boat is wrongfully compelled by another boat to break rule 31.1, she shall be exonerated

(a) if the other boat acknowledges breaking a rule of Part 2 by taking a penalty or retiring immediately, or

(b) under rule 64.1(b), after successfully protesting another boat involved in the same incident.

Rule 31.1

Daisy must not hit a mark: that is to say, she must not touch any object designated by the race committee in the sailing instructions when it has a required side for her. Touch means *no* part of her: a finger tip or a brush of the spinnaker sheet (ISAF 153) invokes the rule. In US 59, a Lightning cleared a mark by some 5 feet, but it was drawn against her hull as she rounded. Although hitting the submerged tackle was not an infringement (see definition Mark), touching the mark itself, for whatever reason, was. We have looked at required sides in rule 28.2. When the sailing instructions state that buoy X must be left to port, X becomes a mark, but X must be looked at from *Daisy*'s viewpoint at any given moment during the race as to whether she may touch it with impunity or not.

She may not touch a starting mark before starting (most commonly, there are two: the committee boat and the pin end buoy). Since she cannot infringe the rule until she is racing and she only begins racing at the preparatory signal, any contacts before then will have no effect. After the start, the starting marks (I presume both of them) begin the leg on which she is sailing – the first leg of the course.

She may not touch a mark that begins, bounds or ends the leg she is on. Just as the mark that began the leg she was on might be a starting mark, so the mark that ends the leg she is on can also be a finishing mark. We have seen in rule 28.2 that this leaves her free to touch a mark that is on another leg of the course from the one she is sailing on.

She may not touch a finishing mark after finishing. We shall see under the definition of finishing exactly what that implies, but among other things it includes clearing the finishing marks. If *Daisy* gets her bow over the line and then drifts against the mark she breaks the rule.

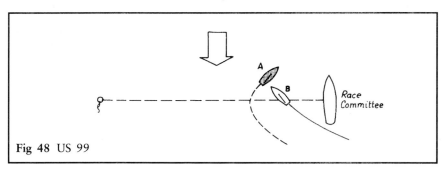

Fig 48 US 99

It is sometimes difficult to determine whether the rule has been broken or not. US 99 (Fig 48) and US 136 (Fig 49) deal with the subject, and the latter states: 'A boat crossing and clearing the middle of the finishing line has also cleared the finishing marks and is no longer racing.' Looking at Fig 49, it is obvious that the boat is well clear of the line and could have switched on her engine (if she had one) without anyone suggesting that she was still racing and therefore not allowed to motor.

Rule 31.2

Having hit the mark and infringed rule 31.1, what can *Daisy* do? Retirement used to be her only choice. She may still retire – and indeed,

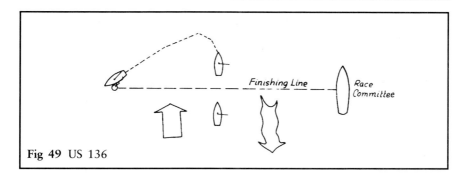

Fig 49 US 136

in crowded waters, some sailing instructions will make her do this – but retirement is not included in the rule because she can take a lesser penalty, or if another boat made her touch she can protest the other boat.

When she knows she is in the wrong she may follow the instructions in rule 31.2 and complete a 360° turn. She must as soon as possible get clear of all other boats and then promptly do her turn. Rule 20 now clarifies a disputed point. She loses her rights of way, but only while she is doing her turn; she keeps them while she is getting clear.

When she hits a starting mark after the preparatory signal she must still do her turn as soon as possible, which effectively grades the severity of the penalty from a minor annoyance at four minutes before the gun, to a real killer at only five seconds to go.

When she hits a finishing mark she must do her turn (on either side of the line), sail until she is completely on the pre-finish side, and then finish. Remember, her string must lie correctly when pulled tight.

We learn in rule 44.4(a) that if *Daisy* has also infringed a rule of Part 2 in the same incident and is 'taking a 720', she need not do a third turn for hitting the mark.

Rule 31.3

It is probable that *Daisy* believes that *Buttercup* has forced her on to the mark and is to blame for the whole incident, and when *Buttercup* admits her mistake and takes a penalty, *Daisy* need do nothing.

However, when *Buttercup* does nothing, or even protests *Daisy*, *Daisy* must lodge a valid protest against a boat involved in the incident (most probably *Buttercup*), and this protest must succeed. The protest must result in another boat in the incident being disqualified. When *Daisy*'s protest is successful she will be exonerated for her infringement of rule 31.1 by rule 64.1(b), but she cannot otherwise escape penalty. Nor will it be enough for *Buttercup* to protest *Daisy*;

Daisy will still be penalized if she has not herself protested according to the rule (ISAF 120).

But beware, *Daisy* must be correct in believing that *Buttercup* took her penalty because of that incident. If in any doubt, she should hail and fly her protest flag and then, on coming ashore, ask *Buttercup* whether she admits her fault; if not, *Daisy* can still lodge her protest in time. In a recent World Championship event two boats hit the committee boat at the start, close together, but in what were in fact two separate incidents. A did a turn; B did not, believing it was one incident, and that A had done a 720° acknowledging fault for everything, but this was not so. Protested by the race committee, B was disqualified.

Rule 32 Shortening or Abandoning After the Start

After the starting signal, the race committee may *abandon* the race (flag N or flag N over H or A) or shorten the course (flag S), as appropriate,

(a) because of an error in the starting procedure,

(b) because of foul weather,

(c) because of insufficient wind making it unlikely that any boat will *finish* within the time limit,

(d) because a *mark* is missing or out of position, or

(e) for any other reason directly affecting the safety or fairness of the competition.

However, after one boat has sailed the course and *finished* within the time limit, if any, the race committee shall not *abandon* the race without considering the consequences for all boats in the race or series.

We have seen under rule 27 the powers and limitations of the race officer before the starting signal; but now his powers are much more limited. This rule allows him to abandon or shorten the race for a few, well-defined circumstances. His discretion is wide – some think too wide – but not unlimited; the situations that permit him to act are:

(a) because of an error in the starting procedure. Rule 30.3 has already allowed him to use a general recall for this purpose, but there may be occasions when, for example, a general recall will bring the black flag rule into force, while abandoning will not have this effect;

(b) because of foul weather – meaning, I presume, that there is some danger to boats, not that it is just a nasty cold rainstorm;

(c) because of insufficient wind to finish in the time limit. RYA 82/17 emphasizes that this discretion is dependent on there being a time limit: 'When there is none, insufficient wind does not constitute grounds for abandoning a race, because when there is no time limit, there must be an intention to continue the race until it is completed, no matter how long that will take';

(d) because a mark is missing or out of position, discussed under rule 34;

(e) for any other reason directly affecting the safety or fairness of the competition. 'Fairness' is a very subjective term, and he will be a clever race officer who manages to abandon because of, say, a wind shift towards the end of a race without arousing someone's wrath. The race officer must act reasonably; unreasonable decisions may lead to redress.

The last sentence of the rule suggests that, if one boat has finished within the time limit – if there is one – there may be a better way of dealing with the matter than abandoning the race, and orders the race committee to consider the consequences. When only one or two boats out of a large fleet have been prejudiced, it is unfair to the rest to abandon the race. There are numerous forms of redress available; these are discussed under rule 64.2.

In ISAF 85, 15 classes sailed the same course. At a certain moment a mark went missing and some boats claimed redress. The race committee abandoned all racing, including two classes that had had no problem. Reinstating the races for these classes, the US Appeals Committee stated that since no claims had been forthcoming of any adverse effect on their competition resulting from the shifted mark, the race committee was not entitled to abandon those two races.

Rule 33 Changing the Course After the Start

> At any rounding *mark* the race committee may signal a change of the direction of the next leg of the course by displaying flag C and the compass bearing of that leg before any boat begins it. The race committee may change the length of the next leg by displaying flag C and a '–' if the leg will be shortened or a '+' if the leg will be lengthened.

Some say that because the rule refers to a rounding mark it cannot be used to change the course at the start/finish line when boats complete a lap. But this is not so. The finishing line is only there, strictly speaking, for boats as they finish; on each lap one of the finishing marks acts as a rounding mark: the rounding mark that ends the previous leg and begins the next leg for each boat. A refinement allows the race officer to add a '+' or a '–' to the board, which is useful in a strengthening or a failing wind.

C requires repetitive flag signals; and it is essential that the signals are loud and given in good time and close enough to be heard.

Rule 34 Mark Missing

> When a *mark* is missing or out of position, the race committee shall, if possible,
>
> (a) replace it in its correct position, or
>
> (b) substitute one of similar appearance, or a buoy or vessel displaying flag M.

No marks – no race! If a mark goes missing, the race committee must put another down if possible. When it is impossible to replace the mark, the race committee can shorten the course if there is still time, or abandon the race. There may be exceptional circumstances when the race can stand; for example, in a long race, if there is a buoy near the position of the missing mark, that all the competitors round, and no one requests redress.

Rule 35 Time Limit

> If one boat sails the course as required in rule 28.1 and *finishes* within the time limit, if any, all boats shall be scored unless the race is *abandoned*. If no boat *finishes* within the time limit, the race committee shall *abandon* the race.

Unless sailing instructions prescribe a time limit there will be none; when they do, and lay down no other rules, once one boat has finished in time, the rest of the fleet has the opportunity to finish even if it takes all night. Often sailing instructions state that once one boat has finished the rest have an hour before the axe falls; those that have not finished by that time are marked DNF. When sailing instructions state that there is no time limit, it is clear that the intention is to sail the race to its bitter end, and the race committee may not abandon because of bad weather.

The rule requires the boat finishing in time to have sailed the course according to rule 29.1. This means that if *Daisy* alone finishes before the time limit, and later she is found to have missed out a mark and is disqualified, the race must then be abandoned. This may well be *very* annoying for those behind, but the rule can of course be altered to fit the circumstances.

In US 199, the race committee got itself into a proper muddle. The Lahaina/Honolulu race consisted of six classes with class trophies and several over-all prizes and trophies. Leading boats in the larger classes finished within the time limit, but none from the smaller. Sorting out the confusion, the US Appeals Committee held that the first boat had made the over-all trophies available to all boats, including those in the smaller classes; but that the trophies for the smaller classes, whose leaders had not finished in time, could not be won. The decision noted that there could have been incongruous results where a D class boat could conceivably have won corrected time honours, yet not participated in a valid race in her own class.

Rule 36 Races to be Restarted or Resailed

> If a race is restarted or resailed, a breach of a *rule*, other than rule 30.3, in the original race shall not prohibit a boat from competing or, except under rule 30.2, 30.3 or 69, cause her to be penalized.

Races can be postponed, abandoned or recalled by a general recall and restarted, or they can be resailed. There is little if any difference between the two, but a restart comes usually immediately after the void start, and a resail is often a few hours or a day later. Rescheduling (see rule 80) is used for races abandoned, and then laid on again some weeks or even months later.

Except for gross misconduct under rule 69 and starting system infringements (rules 30.2 and 30.3), no rule infringements are carried forward and no boat can be penalized. However, we saw under rule 30.3 that this does not prevent a boat being found 'guilty' of an infringement, thus permitting another to get redress under rule 62.1(b).

It is only expressly stated in rule 80, but it is undoubtedly the duty of the race officer to inform the fleet of when and where the race is going to be resailed, and indeed to allow them time to get there. In RYA 69/12, a race officer postponed a race in order to move the starting line. The race was then restarted before two of the boats had time to arrive at the new place. The protest committee refused redress on the grounds that the race officer had not contravened sailing instructions or the racing rules. Upholding the appeal, the RYA said that the race officer acted improperly in laying a fresh starting line and restarting the race without adequately ensuring that all boats could reach the new position and manoeuvre to get a good start, and redress was granted.

(Numbers 37–39 are spare numbers)

Part 4 – Other Requirements When Racing

> *Part 4 rules apply only to boats **racing**.*

Because Part 4 rules only apply when racing, if a race committee wishes one of its rules to apply before the preparatory signal or after a boat has finished, a sailing instruction will be necessary. All Part 4 rules can be altered by sailing instructions, except rule 43. Class rules may alter rules 42 and 49.

Rule 40 Personal Buoyancy

> When flag Y is displayed before or with the warning signal, competitors shall wear life-jackets or other adequate personal buoyancy. Wet suits and dry suits are not adequate personal buoyancy.

When the weather is bad, a race committee cannot always check that each competitor is wearing suitable personal buoyancy; or, when it is worn, whether the equipment is up to standard. It is therefore the individual responsibility of everyone to equip themselves properly and to use their equipment (rule 2). However, competitors can be forced to wear 'life-jackets or other adequate personal buoyancy' when flag Y is flown; they are at risk of being disqualified if they do not. Sailing instructions can increase the time to cover the whole period that boats are afloat – a provision that is often made in order to comply with local authority requirements.

Rule 41 Outside Help

> A boat may receive outside help as provided for in rule 1. Otherwise, she shall not receive help except for an ill or injured crew member or, after a collision, from the crew of the other boat.

Not a screwdriver, nor a spare sheet, not even a sandwich, may be handed over after the preparatory signal; each boat is on her own: she may not receive help from other boats racing, spectators, coaches, or anyone else. There are some exceptions, though.

Rule 1 provides that you may receive help when you or your boat are in danger, or when someone is ill. Equally, if *Daisy* has collided with *Buttercup*, the crews may help each other to get clear. Otherwise, no help may be accepted and except when racing under the team racing appendix (see rule D1.1(d)), you may not help a mate by sitting on, or hindering, someone he wants pushed down the fleet (see ISAF 155). Such a simple rule, you might think, but the decisions are often difficult, especially when dealing with advice and information from modern communications systems. Each case must be decided individually on the basis of its own facts.

It is more difficult when the help is given orally. In RYA 78/1, dinghies were racing in fog and had problems in finding one of the marks. Some motorboats cruising about told an unknown number of boats where it was and the RYA took the view that the rule had not been broken by the advice. This may have been because the advice was given randomly to competitors. Were it, say, a Ruritanian coach advising a Ruritanian boat, the decision would undoubtedly be different.

In an Italian case (FIV 67/5) where, during a cadet race, a coach gave individual advice at a mark, the decision read: 'It is common sense that since competition between individuals must be based on the . . . skill of the competitor, the cases covered by rule 41 should not be limited to purely material help, but must include any suggestion of information furnished during the race to the competitor by a third person which can be considered to have some connection with the competitor himself and which places him who receives it in a position of unfair advantage with respect to the others.' This view has been further confirmed by RYA 93/6, which states: 'While it is possible that a competitor may be fortunate enough, without risk of penalization under rule 41, to learn from comments of spectators that his current intentions are not in his best interests, . . . specific advice given by any person with an interest in the matter, and acted on so as to improve the boat's finishing position, is clearly outside help.'

When organizers wish to be absolutely sure that no boat receives outside help, they must exclude support boats from the race area and ban radios and, of course, telephones; or they may need to lay down rules about the use of private frequencies for weather forecasts etc; wind on the water can be seen from the air and boats directed to it. However, with the proliferation of portable telephones this subject is wide open, and very difficult to manage. There is no ruling, but I imagine that any useful information given privately would be 'outside help', while on a public and publicized frequency it would be acceptable. But what if the information, while available to all, is given in Ruritanian? Would it be 'outside help' to just the Ruritanian entries or must each boat carry a Ruritanian speaker?

But none of this refers to protesting. In US 228, three boats successfully protested a fourth for an illegal daggerboard. The disqualified boat appealed on the grounds that, amongst other things, the protestors were in collusion and thus violated rule 41. The US Appeals Committee decided that it was not contrary to the principle of the rule for several boats to consult about a protest, and then lodge multiple protests or a joint protest.

Rule 42 Propulsion

42.1 Basic Rule

Except when permitted in rule 42.3 or rule 45, a boat shall compete by using only the wind and water to increase, maintain or decrease her speed. Her crew may adjust the trim of sails and hull, and perform other acts of seamanship, but shall not otherwise move their bodies to propel the boat.

42.2 Prohibited Actions

Without limiting the application of rule 42.1, these actions are prohibited:

(a) pumping: repeated fanning of any sail either by trimming and releasing the sail or by vertical or athwartships body movement;

(b) rocking: repeated rolling of the boat, induced either by body movement or adjustment of the sails or centreboard, that does not facilitate steering;

(c) ooching: sudden forward body movement, stopped abruptly;

(d) sculling: repeated movement of the helm not necessary for steering;

(e) repeated tacks or gybes unrelated to changes in the wind or to tactical considerations.

42.3 Exceptions

(a) A boat's crew may move their bodies to exaggerate the rolling that facilitates steering the boat through a tack or a gybe, provided that, just after the tack or gybe is completed, the boat's speed is not greater than it would have been in the absence of the tack or gybe.

(b) Except on a beat to windward, when surfing (rapidly accelerating down the leeward side of a wave) or planing is possible, the boat's crew may pull the sheet and the guy controlling any sail in order to initiate surfing or planing, but only once for each wave or gust of wind.

(c) Any means of propulsion may be used to help a person or another vessel in danger.

(d) To get clear after grounding or colliding with another boat or object, a boat may use force applied by the crew of either boat and any equipment other than a propulsion engine.

Rule 42.1 Basic Rule

The rule places a comprehensive prohibition on such forms of propulsion as engines, oars, paddling with plates – anything except the power provided by wind and water. The crew are limited to 'adjusting the trim of sails and hull' and performing 'other acts of seamanship'; that is to say, those ordinary – or sometimes extraordinary – but necessary acts needed to maximize the effect of the permitted methods of driving the boat forward; acts that may range from reefing or hoisting the spinnaker to pumping out the bilge water. Braking is also controlled: a bailer, for instance, may not be dragged in the water to slow down a dinghy too early at the start. The last phrase bans kinetics. There are detailed prohibitions and exceptions in rules 42.2 and 42.3. (See B4.1 for the sailboard propulsion rule.)

In US 132, a trim tab was fitted and its use in opposition to the rudder, although it slowed the boat, was held not to infringe the rule. It was held to be comparable to backing sails, which does not infringe the rule either.

In ISAF 9, it was decided that throwing an anchor forward and then hauling up on it broke the propulsion rule.

In ISAF 144, a boat switched off her engine at the preparatory signal but still had considerable momentum. It was stated that, 'nothing in the rule requires that a boat be in any particular state of motion or non-motion when she begins racing', so rule 42 was not infringed.

Class rules may alter rule 42 (see rule 86.3), as may sailing instructions, so it can be shaped to order.

Rule 42.2 Prohibited Actions

It is common knowledge that boats can be propelled through the water by judicious movement of weight, or by using the rudder as an oar, or a sail as a fan. Long ago, a gaff-rigged boat could fan her way through a becalmed fleet by continuously gybing her gaff. Today, all small boats and many big ones can be pumped, rocked, ooched or sculled at surprising speeds. When there is little wind, the temptation is great; a good couple of pumps to get ahead of the fleet on the starting line, a little rocking in a flat calm to get round a mark before the tide changes, a sharp spurt out of an awkward spot with a couple of roll tacks: each can ensure a winning position. It is hard for competitors to accept that such acts are just as reprehensible as motoring.

The use of uncontrolled kinetics inevitably would lead to a different sport, and to injuries to the back apparently – hence the efforts to limit them. There are other problems; experienced helmsmen know what they are doing, and it follows that an infringement is almost certainly cheating. It is also infectious; if John pumps and gets away with it, James must do so too or lose all chance of winning. In recognition of the difficulties of policing rule 42, rule 67 allows penalization without a hearing in certain circumstances. Such infringements give rise to scores that cannot be discarded (see rule A1.3).

Major events often use a system of judging on the water, signalling with a yellow flag. The penalty is first a '720', then disqualification, and finally exclusion from the event. It is a system that works well, but only with highly experienced judges who know the class they are judging.

Rule 42.2 prohibits and defines pumping, rocking, ooching, sculling and repeated tacks and gybes; rule 42.3 permits one controlled roll tack or gybe, and allows one pump of any sheet to initiate surfing or planing when conditions are suitable.

There are few recorded cases on this rule. In ISAF 14, a power cruiser, creating large waves, passed a small dinghy reaching at hull speed on a parallel course. As each wave reached his quarter, the helmsman moved his tiller across the centre line in a series of alterations of course rhythmically timed to the passage of the waves under his boat. The US Appeals Committee held that no infringement had taken place: 'Taking advantage of wave action is consistent with rule 42.1. To do so a helmsman may move his tiller as he thinks best.' Furthermore, US 56 points out that 'while A moved his tiller forcefully to starboard several times before reaching the mark and to port several times after that point, he did not bring it amidships . . . the purpose and result of his actions were only to alter the course of his boat and not to give her headway'.

From a protest committee's point of view, rule 42 is notoriously difficult to judge correctly and fairly, and even more difficult to prove any infringement. Careful tape recordings of positions, times, sea state and sail numbers – and descriptions and countings of, say, pumps – will ensure that competitors accept their penalties, even if grudgingly.

Rule 42.3 Exceptions

Rule 42.3(c) makes it clear that you can use any form of propulsion you wish to go to help someone in danger. It is quite common in offshore racing to see a flare at night and to go under power to investigate. This is allowed, and you may also get redress under rule 62.1(c), but make a point of logging your positions and times; obviously you should not lose by your excursion, but you must not gain.

Rule 42.3(d) allows *Daisy*, if she goes ashore or collides with another boat or with an 'object', to use any of her own equipment to get clear except her engine. This may sound odd – she is in danger but cannot use her engine? Well of course she *can* use it, but she must then retire. The reason? The knowledge that she could use her engine to get clear would lead boats to sail nearer and nearer to rocks or other dangers. When two boats collide with each other, the two crews can help each other to get clear.

Rule 43 Competitor Clothing and Equipment

43.1 (a) Competitors shall not wear or carry clothing or equipment for the purpose of increasing their weight.

(b) Furthermore, a competitor's clothing and equipment shall not weigh more than 8 kilograms, excluding a hiking or trapeze harness and clothing (including footwear) worn only below the knee. Class rules or sailing instructions may specify a lower weight or a higher weight up to 10 kilograms. Class rules may include footwear and other clothing worn below the knee within that weight. A hiking or trapeze harness shall have positive buoyancy and shall not weigh more than 2 kilograms, except that class rules may specify a higher weight up to 4 kilograms. Weights shall be determined as required by Appendix J.

(c) When a measurer in charge of weighing clothing and equipment believes a competitor may have broken rule 43.1(a) or rule 43.1(b) he shall report the matter in writing to the protest committee.

43.2 Rule 43.1(b) does not apply to boats required to be equipped with lifelines.

This is an ISAF policy rule which, for reasons of health and safety, seeks to prevent those who weigh little (and indeed those who weigh a lot) ballasting themselves down dangerously with water bottles or lead. The rule may not be altered by national authorities (86.1), while sailing instructions and class rules may permit limited change as stated in the rule itself, and boats with lifelines have rule 43.2 to themselves. Remember rule 43.1 can be broken even within the weight limits of rule 43.1(b).

No cases have reached the case books, possibly because its main use is at championship meetings where there is no appeal from an international jury. Appendix J lays down the methods to be used by measurers checking compliance with the rule. ISAF 170 states that a beverage container cannot be worn except on sailboards. In very hot weather, competitors need to drink, but in anything except a board, water can be stored aboard.

Rule 44 Penalties for Breaking Rules of Part 2

44.1 Taking a Penalty

A boat that may have broken a rule of Part 2 while *racing* may take a penalty at the time of the incident. Her penalty shall be a 720° Turns Penalty unless the sailing instructions specify the use of the Scoring Penalty or some other penalty. However, if she caused serious damage or gained a significant advantage in the race or series by her breach she shall retire.

44.2 720° Turns Penalty

After getting well clear of other boats as soon after the incident as possible, a boat takes a 720° Turns Penalty by promptly making two complete 360° turns (720°) in the same direction, including two tacks and two gybes. When a boat takes the penalty at or near the finishing line, she shall return completely to the course side of the line before *finishing*.

44.3 Scoring Penalty

(a) A boat takes a Scoring Penalty by displaying a yellow flag at the first reasonable opportunity after the incident, keeping it displayed until *finishing,* and calling the race committee's attention to it at the finishing line. At that time she shall also inform the race committee of the identity of the other boat involved in the incident. If this is impracticable, she shall do so at the first reasonable opportunity within the time limit for *protests.*

(b) If a boat displays a yellow flag, she shall also comply with the other parts of rule 44.3(a).

(c) The boat's penalty score shall be the score for the place worse than her actual finishing place by the number of places stated in the sailing instructions, except that she shall not be scored worse than Did Not Finish. When the sailing instructions do not state the number of places, the number shall be the whole number (rounding 0.5 upward) nearest to 20% of the number of boats entered. The scores of other boats shall not be changed; therefore two boats may receive the same score.

44.4 Limits on Penalties

(a) When a boat intends to take a penalty as provided in rule 44.1 and in the same incident has touched a *mark*, she need not take the penalty provided in rule 31.2.

(b) A boat that takes a penalty shall not be penalized further with respect to the same incident unless she failed to retire when rule 44.1 required her to do so.

The rule proposes two penalties, the 720° Turns Penalty and the Scoring Penalty. The first is an automatic default penalty, unless the second, or some other system or none (leading to disqualification), is introduced by sailing instructions. It is commonly believed that only when *Buttercup* hails protest and displays her flag need *Daisy* go and do her turns, but this is not so; *Daisy* must be her own judge of whether or not she has infringed a rule. In RYA 90/8, the RYA stated: 'There is no obligation on a right-of-way boat to protest after an incident. That she does not protest in no way diminishes the fact that the give-way boat has broken a rule.'

The penalty must be taken at once, and the rule does not allow a competitor time to deliberate whether he has broken a rule. If he realizes too late that he has, the penalty is not available (US 280).

Two points will stop *Daisy* getting undue advantage from taking a penalty. If the incident resulted in serious damage (ISAF 154 and 156), or if she gained by her penalty, she must retire – and, of course, if she does not retire she can be disqualified for not doing so.

Rule 44.2 now makes it clear that first a boat sails well clear of the others and then she begins to take her penalty. It was ambiguous, and in a Dragon World event there was a great dispute when a leeward boat, off to do turns, sailed a windward boat a long way from the course. When did the penalty begin and when did L lose her rights? Was she entitled to do what she did? I hope the answer is now clear: L does not lose her rights (rule 20) until she starts to do her turns. This may seem hard on W, but any other arrangement can be dangerous.

Rule 44.4(a) makes the important point that *Daisy* need not do a '720' *and* a '360' if she hits another boat and a mark in the same incident; the '720' is enough.

Rule 44.4(b) ensures that if *Daisy* takes a penalty, protests nevertheless, but then loses the protest, she can be penalized no further; this is a good insurance – depending on the circumstances. It also means that if *Daisy* is disqualified under two rules, say rules 10 and 14, one '720' is enough to exonerate her.

Rule 45 Hauling Out; Making Fast; Anchoring

A boat shall be afloat and off moorings at her preparatory signal. Thereafter, she may not be hauled out or made fast except to bail out, reef sails, or make repairs. She may anchor or the crew may stand on the bottom. She shall recover the anchor before continuing in the race unless she is unable to do so.

You cannot hang on to a convenient mooring buoy near the line and sail off at two seconds to the start. *Daisy* must be afloat and off moorings at her preparatory signal. There are then clear limitations on what she may do.

RYA 62/4 allowed a crew member to stand on a ramp in shallow water, holding the boat that was afloat; had he been standing out of the water, the boat would technically have been made fast by means other than anchoring, moored perhaps.

The anchor must be recovered. I clearly remember a big American yawl anchored 100 yards from the finishing line at Plymouth breakwater, struggling in the early morning breeze to get her anchor up so that she could finish the Fastnet Race, while the minutes of her time allowance slipped by. However, recovery is not always possible, and this is one of the rare occasions where the protest committee is allowed to let a boat off the hook.

Rule 46 Person in Charge

A boat shall have on board a person in charge designated by the member or organization that entered the boat. See rule 75.

It is important for race organizers to know who is in charge of a boat. With large offshore crews they need one person with whom to deal and who is responsible. It used to be the owner, but this is often not the case nowadays when boats may be owned by companies, or all the boats are loaned. Race entry forms should ensure that the name and address of the person in charge are identified. It should be he or she who signs protest forms, and speaks for the boat. To be faced by an owner who disowns the signature of his long-standing and trusted skipper is an embarrassment that once happened to me and is not agreeable. The rule is linked to rule 75 (Entering a Race).

Anyone may steer a boat unless a sailing instruction or some other rule states otherwise (ISAF 90).

Rule 47 Limitations on Equipment and Crew

47.1 A boat shall use only the equipment on board at her preparatory signal.

47.2 No person on board shall leave, unless ill or injured or to help a person or vessel in danger. However, a person leaving the boat by accident or to swim shall be back on board before the boat continues in the race.

Rule 47.1

New equipment may not be taken aboard after the preparatory signal; to do so would be very close to 'outside help'. A coach may be frantic to pass a forgotten but vital sail to a boat, but he must not do so. There is no rule that says *Daisy* must finish with the equipment she started with, except that rule 42.3(d), as we saw, required her to bring home her anchor if possible, and rule 51 might be invoked if a lot of heavy stuff went overboard. However, she may lose a sheet or a sail overboard and not be penalized. Class rules or safety regulations, though, may well require boats to finish with items of gear still aboard.

Rule 47.2

Your crew cannot jump overboard at the last mark, leaving you to sail the greatly lightened boat to victory, but you are allowed to have an enjoyable swim in mid-Atlantic, fall overboard and be rescued and, of course, help others. Case law consists of bizarre cases, unlikely to happen ever again, and it is difficult to draw any interpretations of general application.

Rule 48 Fog Signals and Lights

When safety requires, a boat shall sound fog signals and show lights as required by the International Regulations for Preventing Collisions at Sea or applicable government rules.

This rule is different from the IRPCS rule, which requires lights from sunset to sunrise (this means a different time for each meridian); but the 'When safety requires' phrase is intended to exclude circumstances such as sailing during long northern evenings in isolated waters with no shipping, where a race can safely be finished after sunset without lights.

Rule 49 Crew Position

49.1 A boat shall use no device other than hiking straps to project a competitor's body outboard.

49.2 When lifelines are required by the class rules or the sailing instructions they shall be taut, and competitors shall not position any part of their torsos outside them, except briefly to perform a necessary task. On boats equipped with upper and lower lifelines of wire, a competitor sitting on the deck facing outboard with his waist inside the lower lifeline may have the upper part of his body outside the upper lifeline.

This rule is angled towards the effect of crew weight on stability; it ties in with rule 51. The importance of getting weight to windward can be seen by taking a look at any sportsboat, and trapezes are prohibited unless permitted by class rules. When there are no trapezes, torsos are hung over the side by means of hiking harnesses or, where lifelines prevent that, heavy men are edged out as far as possible.

ISAF 83 (Fig 50) shows three positions that are considered legitimate under this rule, two that are not and one that depends on the type of lifelines. The critical word is 'torso', which has been held not to include arms and legs. Some classes are turning against positions 1 and 4, particularly at night, so competitors should check which regulations govern the race they are about to sail.

In ISAF 162, a spinnaker trimmer stands on the weather deck holding the sheet. Compensating for changes in the boat's trim and the load on the sheet, he is seen to be sometimes leaning back with part of his torso outboard of the lifelines. In answer to a number of questions, the RYA replied that it was clear from diagram 6 of ISAF 83 that he might infringe rule 49. The phrase 'to perform a necessary task' meant that the torso might only be outside the lifeline for some task that could not reasonably be carried out from within the lifelines. The torso must be moved inboard as soon as the task was completed. The rule is aimed at safety as well as stability, and the actions of the crew member were considered to contravene rule 49.

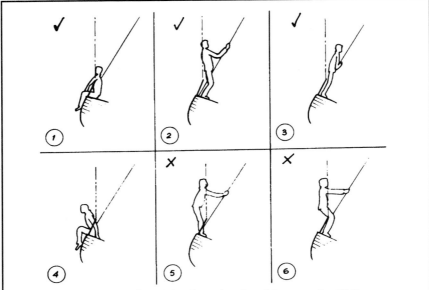

Fig 50 ISAF 83: Note that 4 is allowed only with two wire lifelines.

Rule 50 Setting and Sheeting Sails

50.1   Changing Sails

When headsails or spinnakers are being changed, a replacing sail may be fully set and trimmed before the replaced sail is lowered. However, only one mainsail and, except when changing, only one spinnaker shall be carried set at a time.

50.2   Spinnaker Poles, Whisker Poles

Only one spinnaker pole or whisker pole shall be used at a time except when gybing. When in use, it shall be attached to the foremost mast.

50.3   Use of Outriggers

(a)   No sail shall be sheeted over or through an outrigger, except as permitted in rule 50.3(b). An outrigger is any fitting or other device so placed that it could exert outward pressure on a sheet or sail at a point from which, with the boat upright, a vertical line would fall outside the hull or deck planking. For the purpose of this rule, bulwarks, rails and rubbing strakes are not part of the hull or deck planking and the following are not outriggers: a bowsprit used to secure the tack of a working sail, a bumkin used to sheet the boom of a working sail, or a boom of a boomed headsail that requires no adjustment when tacking.

(b) (1) Any sail may be sheeted to or led above a boom that is regularly used for a working sail and is permanently attached to the mast from which the head of the working sail is set.

(2) A headsail may be sheeted or attached at its clew to a spinnaker pole or whisker pole, provided that a spinnaker is not set.

50.4 Headsails

The difference between a headsail and a spinnaker is that the mid-girth of a headsail, measured from the mid-points of its luff and leech, does not exceed 50% of the length of its foot, and no other intermediate girth exceeds a percentage similarly proportional to its distance from the head of the sail. A sail tacked down behind the foremost mast is not a headsail.

It is frequently suggested that the whole of rule 50 should be removed from the racing rules, being matters for class rules. True, but they serve as class rules for a large number of handicap classes, which have no class rules of their own.

Various cases deal with the details of setting sails. ISAF 7 states that the crew may hold out the sheet of a headsail or spinnaker since a crew member is not an outrigger. US 125 agrees, though here the sheet was held out by a crew's foot. (But be careful what you do with the sheet while you hold it out – do not infringe rule 42, Propulsion.) US 148 saw the mid section of a spinnaker supported in a calm by a paddle, but a paddle was not an outrigger, nor did it extend further than allowed by the rule.

Rule 51 Moving Ballast

All movable ballast shall be properly stowed, and water, dead weight or ballast shall not be moved for the purpose of changing trim or stability. Floorboards, bulkheads, doors, stairs and water tanks shall be left in place and all cabin fixtures kept on board.

The problem of ballast is as old as racing, and only the strictest adherence to these and class rules prevents us going back to the 'sandbaggers' dragging their sand bags from side to side with each tack.

In anything of a wind, *Daisy* sails better with the crew up to windward, she will sail better still if her sails, tool boxes, water, lead ballast, engine etc are also moved up to windward; but while the crew can do what they like, provided they stay inside the lifelines (rule 49), the movement of non-living ballast is forbidden. Because the rule is difficult to police, it has been suggested that it would be a good thing to scrap it; but were it to go we might soon see swinging engines and ballast hauled to windward at each tack and, apart from the expense, a timing error that left all the weight to leeward in a sea might then prove disastrous.

Some newish classes now have water ballast that is pumped from side to side, which is obviously a real help on long offshore legs. This is permissible as long as class rules allow it.

There is no case law, and any infringement that was ever proved was almost certainly dealt with under rule 69 because it was deliberate cheating. It is essential to enforce this rule as strictly as possible and to make newcomers to the sport aware of its existence and importance.

Rule 52 Manual Power

> A boat's standing rigging, running rigging, spars and movable hull appendages shall be adjusted and operated only by manual power.

Rule 53 Skin Friction

> A boat shall not eject or release a substance, such as a polymer, or have specially textured surfaces that could improve the character of the flow of water inside the boundary layer.

Rule 54 Forestays and Headsail Tacks

> Forestays and headsail tacks, except those of spinnaker staysails when the boat is not close-hauled, shall be attached approximately on a boat's centre-line.

Rule 54 was inserted after 1930 to stop a loophole at the KSSS centenary race in Stockholm when a 6-Metre arrived with double headstays and the jib tacked to a curved track on deck. Today, most classes control forestays and track in their own class rules, but the rule serves for those handicap classes that have no class rules of their own.

(Numbers 55–59 are spare numbers)

Part 5 – Protests, Hearings, Misconduct and Appeals

Section A – Protests

Rule 60 Right to Protest and Request Redress

60.1 A boat may

   (a) protest another boat, but not for an alleged breach of a rule of Part 2 unless she was involved in or saw the incident; or

   (b) request redress.

60.2 A race committee may

   (a) protest a boat, but not as a result of a report by a competitor from another boat or other *interested party* or of information in an invalid *protest*;

   (b) request the protest committee to consider giving redress; or

   (c) report to the protest committee requesting action under rule 69.1(a).

60.3 A protest committee may

   (a) protest a boat, but not as a result of a report by a competitor from another boat or other *interested party*, except under rule 61.1(c), nor as a result of information in an invalid *protest*;

   (b) consider giving redress; or

   (c) act under rule 69.1(a).

The rule sets out the basic rights of the various players in the game: the boat, representing the competitors; and those two guardians of discipline and fair play, the race committee and the protest committee.

Rule 60.1
Rule 60.1 allows any boat to protest any other boat with one exception. It has been said that rule 60.1, with only a single exception,

serves to emphasize the broad scope of the right to protest. The right should be liberally interpreted to permit any boat, eligible to race in a series and whose entry has not been rejected or rescinded, to protest . . . whether or not she started in the particular race in question. True, but with an exception for rule 76. In ISAF 2, B infringes a rule in an incident with A, continues to race, and is then involved in another incident with C. Although B is disqualified as a result of the incident with A, her protest against C is still valid. A boat may also protest another in a different race. US 4 confirms this.

The single exception is that *Daisy* must see or be involved in an incident before she can bring a protest under a rule of Part 2. Look at the difference between a Part 2 and a Part 3 protest. After the race, a member of *Daisy*'s crew sees a video in which he sees two incidents of which, until then, he was not aware (see rule 61.1(a)); in the first, P hit the mark, in the second, P ran into S. *Daisy* can now protest P under rule 31 (Part 3) for touching the mark, but not under rule 10, which is in Part 2.

There is no need for a boat to protest if she does not want to; however, as is suggested by 'Sportsmanship and the Rules', there is a moral obligation. We all know protesting is unpopular: it stops the poor owners from going to the cocktail party, it prevents your crew from going home – in other words, it's a bore. Nevertheless, the health of the sport depends on regular steady policing which can usually only be done by competitors. A casual touch of spinnaker on shroud may well be ignored, but dangerous sailing that threatens boats and crews should be stamped on. Turning a blind eye to such behaviour leads to indiscipline and disregard for the rules which, in their turn, lead to cheating and the disintegration of competitive sport.

Rule 60.2

Rule 60.2 deals with the powers of a race committee to discipline its fleet. Just as there is no compulsion on a boat to protest, so there is none on the race committee except in the case of a measurement protest (rule 78.3). There are two limitations.

A race committee may not protest a boat when it has been tipped off by a competitor from another boat or by an interested party. Boats have their own method of getting a protest off the ground, and it would be only too easy for the competitor who knows that he didn't get his flag up in time to bypass his mistake by getting the race committee to do his job for him. 'Interested party' is a defined term, to be identified on the spot – a father, a coach or another competitor will probably all be included in the definition. The second prohibition is on information in invalid protests. If the race committee can act on an invalid protest, its invalidity becomes meaningless. This is a rule that leads to heated arguments.

Subject to these limitations, the race committee is free to protest a boat as it thinks fit. Among other things, it can do something about damage to boat or crew; it can act if it sees an infringement; and it can act on a report from a disinterested witness (one not prohibited above). Competitors must accept that a race committee does not have to act. It has the right to initiate proceedings and disqualify a boat under rule 60.2, but it has no duty to do so. It is sometimes better to ignore minor infringements that have no effect on the speed of a boat. That said, competitors would soon lose respect for a committee that did not use its powers to run fair disciplined racing.

There are other things a race committee can do. It can ask the protest committee to give redress, a very common occurrence where boats have been to help others; and it can take action under rule 69, the gross misconduct rule, but only to the extent that it writes a report to the protest committee which then decides whether to act or not.

Rule 60.3

The protest committee has similar powers and limitations to the race committee, with two exceptions: when during a protest hearing the protest committee realizes from the evidence that the incident between A and B was caused by C, it has the power to protest C and join her to the hearing (ISAF 92). It can also act under rule 69 by starting a hearing of its own accord. In fact, with the exception of protest committee members out on the water acting under rule 67, it is extremely rare in my experience for a protest committee to protest a boat. Unless there is a jury, the protest committee members are usually in their offices or mowing the lawn while the racing is on. Quite rightly, many juries are loath to act on their own. The late Beppe Croce, President of the IYRU, would never look at the last few seconds of a start when he was on a jury so that he would not be influenced by his own impressions.

The protest committee can start redress proceedings and can act under rule 69.1.

Rule 61 Protest Requirements

61.1 Informing the Protestee

(a) A boat intending to protest because of an incident occurring in the racing area that she is aware of shall hail 'Protest' and conspicuously display a red flag at the first reasonable opportunity for each. She shall display the flag either until she *finishes* or retires, or, if the incident occurs near the finishing line, until the race committee acknowledges seeing her flag. In all other cases she shall inform the other boat as soon as reasonably possible.

(b) A race committee or protest committee intending to protest a boat under rule 60.2(a) or rule 60.3(a) because of an incident it observes in the racing area shall inform her after the race within the time limit determined by rule 61.3. In all other cases it shall inform her as soon as reasonably possible.

(c) During the hearing of a valid *protest*, if the protest committee decides to protest a boat that was involved in the incident but is not a *party* to that hearing, it shall inform the boat as soon as reasonably possible of its intention and of the time and place of the hearing.

61.2 Protest Contents
A *protest* shall be in writing and identify

(a) the protestor and protestee;

(b) the incident, including where and when it occurred;

(c) any *rule* the protestor believes was broken; and

(d) the name of the protestor's representative.

Provided the written *protest* identifies the incident, other details may be corrected before or during the hearing.

61.3 Protest Time Limit
A *protest* by a boat, or by the race committee or protest committee about an incident the committee observes in the racing area, shall be delivered to the race office no later than the time limit stated in the sailing instructions. If none is stated, the time limit is two hours after the last boat in the race *finishes*. Other race committee or protest committee *protests* shall be delivered to the race office within two hours after the committee receives the relevant information. The protest committee shall extend the time if there is good reason to do so.

Rule 61.1 *Informing the Protestee*
Rule 61.1(a) When *Daisy* is directly involved in an incident in the racing area and wishes to protest, her helmsman or crew will hail 'Protest' and put up a red flag, each action at the first reasonable opportunity.

1 The words 'Do your turns' or 'I'll see you later' will not do. The word is 'protest'. Shout it as loud as you can. The human voice travels a long way, and, except with large boats in a high wind when the sails and rigging make a deafening noise, your hail will be capable of being heard. Whether the protestee will hear it depends on certain factors; someone concentrating very hard may shut out all exterior sights and sounds. However, this does not matter; you have to shout it, he does not have to hear it. The first reasonable opportunity for the hail will normally be immediately. You may have capsized and be under the water, or you may have the spinnaker wrapped round your head, but usually you can shout at once.

2 The flag must be red, and since flags are normally rectangular, it will be either rectangular or flag B, which by its very definition is a flag. ISAF 147 answers the question 'What is a flag?': 'A flag is used as a signal to visually communicate the message "I intend to protest". Only if the object used as a flag communicates that message, with little or no possibility of causing confusion to other boats, will the object qualify as a flag. A flag must be seen primarily as a flag.' US 297 states that a 2×8 inch flag on a 40 foot boat is not adequate – it would hardly be adequate in an Optimist. A broad interpretation might include a red handkerchief, but not permit a sock, a hat or a jacket.

The first reasonable opportunity for the flag will be later than for the hail, even if only by a second or two.

RYA 83/4 concerns an incident at the gybe mark in the Fireball Worlds. The boats were planing on and off to the leeward mark where the protest flag was at last displayed. The protest was held to be invalid, and on appeal this was confirmed. The flag was flown at the first convenient opportunity, not the first reasonable opportunity.

Whether or not the flag has been flown in time is a matter for the protest committee to decide. Committees will be sympathetic when a protesting boat would clearly have lost places if she had struggled with a flag, but although excuses (or reasons) for not displaying the flag within a moment or two of the incident are many and varied, few succeed.

If the incident is near the finishing line, *Daisy* must keep her flag up until it is acknowledged by the race committee, otherwise she can take it down when she finishes or retires. However, she will be wise to try and make sure that the race officer has seen it, for his evidence may be useful at the protest hearing. Many sailing instructions require the boat to have her flag acknowledged, and anyway it is always courteous to tell the race officer that you are going to protest. If you tell him by radio you can name the other party, then he can warn the shore and you may well get your protest heard half an hour earlier.

When *Daisy* wishes to protest an incident between *Buttercup* and *Tulip*, she must hail and display her protest flag as if she were involved in the incident herself (US 67).

The sailboard appendix waives the requirement for a protest flag, but still asks for the hail (rule B5).

Rule 61.1(b) No flag or hail is needed for a committee, race or protest, but it is subject to the same time limits as a protesting boat (see rule 61.3), and should tell the boat concerned as soon as possible that she is being protested. This does not mean a committee boat rushing into a mêlée of boats at a mark in order to shout a warning, but if the boat comes near at the end of the race she should be hailed.

Rule 61.1(c) We have already seen under rule 60 that if a protest committee realizes during the hearing of a valid protest that *Daisy*, a boat other than the protestor and protestee, has probably broken a rule, it may protest her. She will have the same rights as any other party to the protest and must be informed and given time (though probably not much) to get her defence together. Since the realization comes during a hearing, the sooner the protest committee can decide to join the third party to the proceedings the better, because the hearing will have to be started all over again, the new boat having the right to hear all the evidence, etc. On these occasions the protest committee should fill in a protest form, thus recording their action against *Daisy*.

Rule 61.2 *Protest Contents*
There is no need for an official form, unless sailing instructions ask for one, but the protest must be in writing and there are certain essentials listed. While most errors or omissions can be corrected before (or even during) the hearing, the protest must identify the incident, otherwise it would be only too easy to make up the story as the hearing proceeded. Note particularly that the protested boat must be identified. This can be difficult for a boat at a crowded mark where sail numbers are often invisible and 'a red hat and yellow jacket' are hardly unique, but without old rule 33 (the contact and protest rule) at least the thwarted protestor does not risk disqualification.

Often there is not much time to write out the protest, but protestors will find it worthwhile to spend a little time on the diagram and, however brief, the description of the incident. A diagram is not essential, but a sensible protestor will make one. If, for example, everything depends on there having been no overlap at the mark and the original sketch shows the boats overlapped, then the case is inevitably weakened despite any later correction. Protests should not be refused for mere technicalities in form filling, but, equally, protestee and protest committee alike must be aware of what the protestor is alleging.

In RYA 85/2, the protestor provided inadequate data, no diagram, and no description of the incident; the rule cited was 36, but there was no indication as to whether the boats were beating or running, or as to what action either of them had taken. The protest was held to be invalid.

Rule 61.3 Protest Time Limit

The time limit for protests and requests for redress is usually governed by sailing instructions, but if these are silent then 'protest time' runs for two hours from when the last boat in the class finished. Often, particularly in offshore racing, this is altered to an individual time of two hours from each boat's finishing time, and if *Daisy* retires but still wants to protest, she will lodge any protest as soon as possible and the protest committee will decide what was reasonable. The race committee also has to get its protest in in time, but this may be difficult if there are a number of classes and the protestor is in the first class to finish. But do not despair, either sailing instructions will have altered 'after the last boat in the race finishes' to 'after the last boat in the last race of the day finishes', or the protest committee will extend the time limit when it is clear that the race officer could not have got his protest in earlier.

This is a great change for race and protest committees, for they used to have a long time in which to act. Now they must (as they usually did) act promptly. Any sensible race officer wishing to protest will in any case call the shore and tell the office of an impending protest. The protestee can then be informed and everyone can start to prepare for a hearing.

The final sentence requires the protest committee to extend the time limit for delivering a protest 'if there is good reason to do so'. It is easy to see that a protest committee must extend the time if, say, a boat breaks her mast and has trouble getting home, and an extension unreasonably refused can be appealed. On the other hand, 'I was having a drink at the bar' would not be a good reason! US 219, discussing the point, stresses the need for reasonableness.

Rule 62 Redress

> **62.1** A request for redress shall be based on a claim that a boat's finishing place in a race or series has, through no fault of her own, been made significantly worse by
>
> (a) an improper action or omission of the race committee or protest committee,

(b) physical damage because of the action of a boat that was breaking a rule of Part 2 or of a vessel not *racing* that was required to keep clear,

(c) giving help (except to herself or her crew) in compliance with rule 1.1, or

(d) a boat against which a penalty has been imposed under rule 2 or disciplinary action has been taken under rule 69.1(b).

62.2 The request shall be made in writing within the time limit of rule 61.3 or within two hours of the relevant incident, whichever is later. No protest flag is required.

Rule 60.1(a) gives boats the right to ask for redress while rules 60.2(b) and 60.3(b) allow race and protest committees to start redress proceedings in favour of a boat (most commonly when she has helped another).

Rule 62 should be read in conjunction with rule 64.2. No protest flag is needed before asking for redress, but in fact a flag can sometimes be a useful and timely piece of evidence of the existence of a problem.

This rule is designed to help *Daisy* when her placing in the results has been adversely affected by one of four things: a mistake by the race or protest committee; being damaged by a vessel required to keep clear or a boat racing that broke a rule; the time she has spent helping others in distress; and being done down by the bad behaviour of another competitor. There are two prerequisites common to all four categories: first, *Daisy*'s finishing position must have been made 'significantly worse' and, secondly, the worsening of her position must have been through no fault of her own.

ISAF 95 states: 'A boat may not protest a race committee for breaking a rule.' Sailing instruction 18 provided for the starting line and first mark to be laid such that the first leg would be sailed to windward. After the race committee did so and had started one class, the wind backed some 55 degrees. The Finn class was next to start, but the first mark could not be moved, since the previous class was still sailing towards it and was well short of it. When the Finns started, none could fetch the first mark on a single tack, but subsequent further backing of the wind permitted some to do so. Boat A requested redress, holding that, under rule 85 and the definition Rule, sailing instruction 18 ranked as a rule, which the race committee had broken.

The protest committee ruled that the results of the race were to stand, and A appealed. Her protest, she said, had not been based on a claim for redress under rule 62, but simply on the fact that the race committee had failed to comply with sailing instruction 18, which was a rule. The RYA upheld the protest committee, saying: 'A boat may request redress, but only on the grounds that, through no fault of her own, an improper act or omission of the race committee made her finishing position significantly worse. The racing rules do not permit a race committee to be protested or penalized.'

A winning boat will not get redress when others have suffered, but she has not. Although *Daisy* won the race, it would pay her points-wise to get the race abandoned for a mistake by the race committee, but she will not achieve this because her finishing position has not been worsened by that mistake. In RYA 89/11, a race started very late and, in spite of a breeze, ran out of time. When the time limit was reached, the race committee took no action, made no signals, timed in the boats, and put up the results. All were happy except one boat which, when she failed to get a gun, realized she had been over the line at the start. Her claim for redress on the grounds that the race committee had to respect the time limit was refused, for her finishing position (OCS) had not been worsened by the race committee error in not abandoning the race.

Rule 62.1 (a) It is only too easy for the best of race committees to make mistakes; the scope is large and the errors very varied: drifting marks, incorrect flag hoists, ambiguous sailing instructions, to name but three. The 'action or omission' of the race or protest committee must be 'improper'. ISAF 123, a case where a measurement authority invalidated a rating certificate, states: 'no action or omission of the race committee was responsible for the error or for its remaining undiscovered, and therefore the boat was not entitled to redress'. This does not mean that because a race officer has acted within the powers given him by, say, rules 27 and 32, no redress will be due. He may act legitimately yet stupidly, mistakenly, or even with bias; and such actions must be redressed when a boat has suffered thereby. Look at RYA 69/12. Fifteen minutes before the preparatory signal the race officer moved the line. He then started the race before all the boats could reasonably have been expected to arrive at the new starting line. He contravened neither the rules nor the sailing instructions, but his actions were manifestly unfair and redress was given.

It is a fairly common mistake to believe that when the race committee has done something wrong the race is automatically 'null and void'. It is nothing of the sort, and indeed rule 32 specifically forbids the abandonment of a race after one boat has finished without considering if it is the fairest thing to do.

The commonest (and often the most difficult) requests for redress are those by boats scored OCS – on the course side of the line (or, as we may come to call them, 'oxes' or even 'oxen'). There is little or no case law, the rules are clear, but juries will know only too well the problem of getting facts. When the race officer or officers are sure, then the boat will need very good evidence to upset the decision to score her OCS; the problems arise when one of the race officers has doubts, or indeed has not seen clearly. In a recent event, the race officer said he was not sure and the jury reinstated the boat, but no sooner were the results up than the race committee asked for the case to be reopened; a mass of evidence from no less than six respected coaches, who had all been sitting on the line at the start, left the jury in no doubt that it had made a mistake and the boat was out. As so often, we believed that this was almost certainly a case for rule 69 (Gross Misconduct), but there was no way of proving it. It is sometimes harder to judge when the boat agrees she was over, but says she came back over the line. The race committee then has to make the jury believe that she did not, and proving a negative is always very difficult.

Let us look at some of the other cases. 'It is not the mistake that is actionable but the fact that the mistake has prejudiced one or more boats'; in RYA 82/3, the starting signal was made one minute early, but the race (unwisely) was allowed to continue. Neither of the two boats requesting redress was affected by the mistake. Their appeal was dismissed. RYA 89/11 is another good example where the race committee made a mistake, but the only boat that requested redress was not prejudiced.

In US 209, the committee started a race in winds that one of the competing Sunfish considered too strong. She chose not to start and then claimed that her finishing position had been significantly worsened by 'starting the race under the existing wind and sea conditions and jeopardizing the safety of competitors'. Her request for redress was refused, a decision confirmed on appeal. 'The decision to start, postpone or abandon a race is solely within the jurisdiction of the race committee. Rule 62 should not be interpreted to restrict or interfere with its authority and responsibilities in matters of race management.' CYA 81 also takes the view that when a boat decides not to race she cannot claim that her finishing position has been affected.

In RYA 89/10, the outer distance mark was moored by cordage of a semi-floating variety that was too long when used in shallow areas, so the surplus was usually tied in a bunch. On this occasion, the bunch came loose and entangled a boat that was finishing. Redress was granted; 'Marks,' said the RYA, 'are laid for the benefit of competing boats and it is important the ground tackle be arranged to minimize the possibility of being fouled. In cases involving errors by the race committee it is a good principle that any doubts be resolved for the benefit of the boats.'

It is a good moment to look briefly at the position of the race officer. He is not an interested party; no redress given or not given will win or lose him any places in the race. Nor will it cost him money; his interest is purely to be as fair as possible to all the fleet. But of course we all know that when we are race officers, our pride can be hurt. We have acted on what we saw, we have done what we thought right, and now someone is saying we were wrong. It is for this reason that in a rule 62.1(a) hearing where the race committee is one of the parties, it is preferable not to have its members sitting on the protest committee. This cannot always be avoided, and of course the race officer may (and probably will) appear as a witness.

Redress can also be sought from the improper action or omission of a protest committee. Normally this only happens when a protest committee, in granting redress to some boats, harms the positions of others who have not been parties to the protest. These boats may seek redress in their turn against the decision, and indeed must do so if they are to have any hope of appealing. If they are right, it means that the protest committee has not heard all the evidence at the first hearing, has come to a mistaken result, and needs to take another look at the case. (ISAF 119, which lays this down, is discussed under rules 64.2 and 70.)

Note that it will always be fruitless to seek redress because of the decision of a protest committee to disqualify a boat that has broken a rule.

Rule 62.1(b) Since the rule's inception in 1961 we have had 'disabled', then 'damaged', and now 'physical damage' – variations that seem to have made little change to the effects of the rule. A few things are clear: *Daisy* must be damaged, yes, but a deep scratch that allows her to sail on will not materially worsen her finishing position and so will not be enough.

The rule deals with racing and non-racing boats. In the first case, *Daisy* may be badly damaged by a give-way boat before the preparatory signal, and although the other boat will not be penalized (preamble to Part 2), *Daisy* will get her redress provided there has been a protest, hearing and decision to show that the other boat had broken a rule.

The rule also covers damage caused by 'a vessel not racing'. Thus redress can be granted for damage by a spectator craft or a committee boat, to name but two. In Australia, a jury has held a helicopter to be a vessel, an understandable decision in these days of gunships; it would be intolerable if a boat were to lose a championship because of over-enthusiastic film makers.

RYA 94/6 makes it clear that it is the action of the other boat that causes the damage; it need not be the boat herself: A was racing, B was under power; there was no collision between the two, but A, in bearing away to avoid B, hit a big steel buoy and was holed. She received redress.

Rule 62.1(c) Rule 1.1 commands *Daisy* to go to the help of any 'person or vessel in danger', when this is possible. It is therefore only fair that she should have redress for her pains. The decision in ISAF 38 shows how unrestrictedly race and protest committees are to interpret rule 1: 'A boat in a position to help another that may be in danger is bound to do so. That a protest committee, assessing later the many factors that may cause a vessel or person to be in danger, concludes that help was offered but not requested and that no danger existed, is irrelevant.' It will also be irrelevant when adjudicating on redress.

In offshore races there are numerous occasions each year when one boat stands by another, perhaps rudderless or without her mast, until satisfied that all is well. On finishing, the rescuer requests redress and her elapsed time is then usually shortened as appropriate. Such decisions can affect the results and must be arrived at with meticulous care: positions, weather, tides – every detail you can think of may affect the outcome. I will tell only one tale out of hundreds. Many years ago in a One Ton Cup, a blazing motorboat was seen at night. A number of competitors went to the rescue, and *Gumboots*, then leading on points, picked up a shipwrecked family from their liferaft. She intended to finish the race, but in the early hours of the morning a child was taken ill and had to be taken ashore. It took three days to work out the various redress claims, but when *Gumboots* was awarded her position at the last mark before the incident, it was good enough to give her the championship.

The rule excludes a boat getting redress for 'self-help'; a boat is not entitled to redress for helping herself or her own crew.

Rule 62.1(d) When *Daisy* is the victim of foul play she may seek redress, but only when the offending boat (or competitor) has been found guilty of breaking rule 2 (Fair Sailing) or has been penalized under rule 69. In ISAF 78, A harassed B throughout the last race of a championship. A was thrown out of the series under rule 69, but there was no redress for B. The introduction of this rule since then would now allow B redress, provided she could show that her finishing position had suffered as a result of A's actions.

Section B – Hearings and Decisions

Rule 63 Hearings

63.1 **Requirement for a Hearing**

A boat or competitor shall not be penalized without a hearing, except as provided in rules 30.2, 30.3, 67 and A1.1. A decision on redress shall not be made without a hearing. The protest committee shall hear all *protests* that have been delivered to the race office unless it approves a protestor's request to withdraw the *protest*.

63.2 **Time and Place of the Hearing**

All *parties* to the hearing shall be notified of the time and place of the hearing, the *protest* or redress information shall be made available to them, and they shall be allowed reasonable time to prepare for the hearing.

63.3 **Right to Be Present**

(a) The *parties* to the hearing, or a representative of each, have the right to be present throughout the hearing of all the evidence. When the *protest* claims a breach of a rule of Part 2, Part 3 or Part 4, the representatives of boats shall have been on board at the time of the incident, unless there is good reason for the protest committee to rule otherwise. Any witness, other than a member of the protest committee, shall be excluded except when giving evidence.

(b) If a *party* to the hearing does not come to the hearing, the protest committee may nevertheless decide the *protest*. If the *party* was unavoidably absent, the committee may reopen the hearing.

63.4 **Interested Party**

A member of a protest committee who is an *interested party* shall not take any further part in the hearing but may appear as a witness. A *party* to the hearing who believes a member of the protest committee is an *interested party* shall object as soon as possible.

63.5 **Validity of the Protest**

At the beginning of the hearing the protest committee shall decide whether all requirements for the *protest* have been met, after first taking any evidence it considers necessary. If all requirements have been met, the *protest* is valid and the hearing shall be continued. If not, it shall be closed.

63.6 **Taking Evidence and Finding Facts**

The protest committee shall take the evidence of the *parties* to the hearing and of their witnesses and other evidence it considers necessary. A member of the protest committee who saw the incident may give evidence. A *party* to the hearing may question any person who gives evidence. The committee shall then find the facts and base its decision on them.

63.7   Protests Between Boats in Different Races
A *protest* between boats sailing in different races conducted by different organizing authorities shall be heard by a protest committee acceptable to those authorities.

Section B provides a framework for handling protests from the moment a protestor gives in his protest form to the race office until, after the hearing, a party (probably a would-be appellant) asks for and is supplied with the protest committee's decision in writing. Procedure may vary slightly from place to place, but certain basic rights remain constant, such as the right to state one's case, to question witnesses, and to be judged by unbiased protest committees. Sailing instructions may alter this section provided that there is a clear and specific reference to the alterations (rule 86.1(b)), but such changes should be made only when it is essential to do so and without prejudicing the competitor.

Incorrect procedure can be appealed, but it is safe to say that, in general, an appeals committee will not upset a decision when the appellant neither raised an objection at the time nor has been harmed by the mistake. Appendix P, Recommendations for Protest Committees, is designed to help those who rarely have the chance to hear protests, and thus may be unfamiliar with normal procedure. The appendix is only consultative, but it is advisable not to disregard it without good reason.

Rule 63.1 Requirement for a Hearing

This rule is a main pillar of the system, and must be remembered when using rule 64.1(a). Time and again a race committee, seeing an obvious infringement, penalizes without giving the boat a hearing and then has an appeal on its hands. A hearing is essential except that a boat may be penalized without a hearing when:

1 under rule 30, either the Z or the black flag starting system is in force and is infringed;

2 under rule 67, when, after notification in sailing instructions, a protest committee member (*not* a member of the race committee) sees an infringement of the propulsion rule;

3 under rule A1.1, when a boat fails to start or finish, she can be scored so (not really a penalty);

4 under Appendices C and D, with umpiring on the water.

Redress requests must be heard too. If a boat lodges a timely, formal request for redress it must be dealt with formally. This may sound unnecessary. Of course, you think, she must be given half an hour off her elapsed Fastnet time for standing by, no need for red tape. But you may be sure that if you just alter her elapsed time you will find that it makes her first, or gives her some prestigious trophy, and other boats will come furiously steaming up, and you have to start over again. Let the protest committee hear the request, take the evidence, and get it right the first time.

All protests lodged must be heard, otherwise the protest committee is not doing its duty, but a lodged protest may be withdrawn, with protest committee permission. I believe that it is a discretion that a protest committee should use very carefully. A and B collide. A lodges a valid protest. B's protest is invalid. Before the protest, A (believing in her heart of hearts that she was wrong) asks to withdraw the protest. My answer would be 'no'. A's reasons for wanting to withdraw must be carefully scrutinized.

Occasionally, the stringent requirements of rule 63.1 are modified by sailing instructions. For example, when all boats come into the same harbour after racing it is easy for the race committee to protest them in the normal way, but when they scatter, each going to her own marina, it may be more satisfactory to penalize *Daisy* summarily for petty infringements of special regulations (navigation lights not showing perhaps). If she does not accept the justice of the penalty, she may always have a hearing on request. Such arrangements are useful, but to be employed sparingly.

Rule 63.2 Time and Place of the Hearing
It is the responsibility of a boat to make sure her witnesses are at the protest room at the right time, though this may be difficult. Sailors often think that protest committees don't care how long they and their witnesses are kept waiting. This is untrue – a lot of juggling goes on to try to minimize the waiting time. Faced by eight protests, I allow 40 minutes for each; this works fairly well – give or take some cases collapsing, and others going on and on and on. Always make sure that the protestee has seen the protest form. If there has been a slip-up and he has not had a photocopy, give him at least five minutes to read it in peace. In RYA 68/15, the protest was available for inspection and was then read out three times; the protestee made no complaint at the hearing nor did she ask for time to prepare her defence. She lost her appeal.

Rule 63.3 *Right to Be Present*

When the protest alleges an infringement of Part 2, Part 3 or Part 4 (ie an on-the-water incident), boats' representatives must have been aboard at the time. (Naturally, there is a let-out clause to this, and the protest committee may accept someone who was not on board – for instance, there might be circumstances when it is desirable for a non-racing owner to represent his own boat.) A boat's representative will normally be the owner and skipper; sometimes he will be the 'person in charge' (see rule 46); or he may simply be appointed by the owner or person in charge as being the best person to argue the case. The chief race officer will represent the race committee whenever possible. A competitor is usually the party in a rule 69 hearing (Gross Misconduct).

Each party may have an interpreter if they so wish; witnesses are excluded until, one at a time, they give their evidence. If you are asked to allow in someone's lawyer, don't automatically say no. There are rare occasions when it is better to let the lawyer hear the true story, rather than his client's garbled version of it. The protest committee may invite observers.

The parties (as defined) or a representative of each have a right to be present in the protest room from the beginning to the end (except while the jury is deliberating); they also have the right to be present at any postponed or adjourned hearing, at a reopening (rule 66), or at a re-hearing when one is ordered by a national authority after an appeal (rule 71.2).

Rule 63.4 *Interested Party*

The definition identifies an interested party, and here we must look at the restraints on such a person. If one of the protest committee members is discovered to be an interested party, he must not take part in the hearing other than to give evidence. The word 'further' is confusing as it implies that someone is already serving on the committee when he is found to be an interested party, and that he must then stop. This is certainly so; but even if not expressly forbidden, it is not desirable for those interested in a result to sit at all. But one thing is sure – anyone who wants to object must do so as soon as possible. You will get no sympathy if, at the end of a hearing, you disclose what you have known all along: that one of the protest committee and the pretty protestee are in fact father and daughter.

Sometimes protest committee members are 'interested'. In RYA 84/2, a Laser sought redress after finishing incorrectly owing to an ambiguity in the sailing instructions. Redress was refused and she appealed, claiming – among other things – that the chairman of the protest committee had competed in the race. This was a fact that she had at first accepted, but then it was learned that he had won his class. Upholding the appeal, the RYA said: 'It is accepted that sometimes, unavoidably, fellow competitors sit on a protest committee, but it is nevertheless undesirable. This is particularly so at redress hearings where the granting or not of redress must potentially affect ... all competitors [who] become, to a greater or lesser extent, interested parties. The chairman of the protest committee in this case would have been well advised to refrain from serving on it. An interested party does not cease to be such because a party to the protest is willing to accept him as a member of the protest committee.'

Naturally, an interested party may give evidence – indeed most pertinent evidence is given by interested parties (the protestor, the protestee and their crews). In theory, members of the race committee are not interested parties; at least they do not stand to gain or lose, nor will they normally have a close personal interest in the result (see rule 62.1(a) and 'interested party').

Rule 63.5 Validity of the Protest

The first job in any hearing is to determine the validity of the protest, or of the request for redress. The protest form should already have written on it the time it was accepted at race headquarters and when protest time ended. If it was timely, go ahead; if it was late, then find out why and, when the excuse is a good one, extend the time limit as laid down by rule 61.3. Redress is subject to the same time limits (rule 62.2).

Now check the protest form to make sure that it describes the incident and identifies the protestee (rule 61.2); the rest can now be corrected as necessary. This is rarely observed, but permissive protest committee attitude can, on appeal, rebound on the protestor, and it does not take much time to add a few words. A protest committee may not reject a protest because the rule alleged to have been broken was not the right one (ISAF 44). Until the facts are known, it is not always possible to pick the right rule.

And finally, most difficult of all, check the hail and the flag (rule 61.3). When the protestor states on his form that the hail has been given and the flag flown in proper time, when the race committee confirms that the flag was flown at the finish and when the protestee has raised no objection, the protest committee may declare the protest valid and go ahead with the hearing. Appeals on the validity of the protest usually fail when no objection has been made at this time.

The fact that the protestee neither heard the hail nor saw the flag does not mean that the hail was not given nor the flag flown. Neither does it necessarily mean that the protestee is lying; it is quite possible for the intense concentration necessary for passing marks in a big fleet to exclude subsidiary information coming into the brain. In addition, the noise is often such that hearing is difficult.

When one or more points are not clear, evidence, if there is any, must be heard from the parties and others. When the protest committee decides that the protest is invalid, it must not be heard nor the information on it used (rules 60.2(a) and 60.3(a)).

Rule 63.6 *Taking Evidence and Finding Facts*

The taking of evidence is an art. If this were not so, lawyers would not command such high fees! To start with, it is difficult to grasp the fundamental situation clearly so that the correct question can be asked. All too frequently, at the end of the hearing a jury member says: 'but we never found out whether she luffed', or 'we never asked the speed of the boats'. With hindsight, it seems impossible that such obvious questions could have been missed, and one begins to appreciate counsels' skill. Never be afraid to recall witnesses or parties to answer another question, but remember that if a witness returns, then so must the parties, then they can hear what he says and question him if they want to. It never ceases to amaze me to read an appeal where the protest committee has omitted to discover whether the inside boat at a mark had established an overlap in proper time or not.

Theoretically, a strict question and answer routine should take place in turn between the parties and the protest committee, but in fact all those present are usually inexperienced interrogators and, provided the chairman keeps complete control, it is often possible to get the two competitors discussing the incident freely. The more relaxed they become, the more likely it is that they will say something of use to the listening judges.

How many witnesses? Since time is short, must all the witnesses be heard? US 54 tried to answer this question in a case where the protest committee, because the prize-giving was held up, had allowed the parties only one witness each, to which the protestor objected that he had four witnesses waiting to testify: two from his boat, and two independent competitors who had seen the incident. 'A protest committee may be justified in exceptional circumstances,' went the decision, 'in declining to hear an indefinite number of witnesses . . . all of whom are prepared to testify to the same set of facts . . . But it was obligated to permit the protestor to present a reasonable number of witnesses waiting to be heard . . . None of these obligations was met, and rule 63.5 was infringed.' There is another viewpoint: if you listen to each of, say, six crew, it is unlikely that they will all tell the same tale, and one may come out with quite unexpected evidence that throws new light (maybe even the truth!) on the whole incident. A firm chairman can both strictly limit the time a witness takes and, by his manner, discourage the party from bringing more witnesses in order to repeat the same story. When a party to the protest asks, 'Do you want to hear my crew?', the answer must be: 'It is your decision, not ours, to call them or not.' In RYA 84/14, one of the parties appealed because her witness was not called, but it was held that the responsibility to call a witness rested with the party and not the protest committee.

The protest committee itself is free to call whom it will. It need not go around hunting for witnesses, but it should protect the interests of all competitors by calling useful witnesses who have been overlooked, sometimes deliberately, by the parties.

Hearsay evidence The rules of hearsay evidence prevent what one person said being reported by another. It is not permitted in law courts (in English law, at any rate), hence the policeman's awkward phrase: 'I spoke to the bartender and, as a result of what he told me, I proceeded to the harbour.' I do not suggest that the complicated rules of hearsay evidence be applied rigidly to protests, but remember that when a protestor says, 'My crew said the distance was 6 feet', it is not acceptable evidence. Indeed, the crew, when he appears as a witness, frequently says something quite different, such as: 'I couldn't see, I was behind the genoa.' Never take such reported evidence when it is possible to call the persons concerned and, when they are not available, largely discount its value. However, when discussing the validity of the protest, a statement such as 'The protestor did not hail "Protest"; he shouted "My main is torn"' is not hearsay, it is direct evidence about the incident.

Leading questions A leading question is not an important question, as many seem to think; instead, it is a question that leads the person questioned to give the required answer. 'You then pulled in your mainsail, didn't you?' expects the answer 'yes', and in this way a witness can be led to produce the wanted answer. In court, a lawyer may not lead his client for obvious reasons; he may only lead when cross-examining his opponent's witnesses. Again, with untrained people on each side of the table, the legal rules cannot be rigidly applied, but a warning if a party begins to lead his witness can be enough. Otherwise the evidence is virtually useless. 'Would you say that the distance between the boats at that moment was about 6 feet?' asks the helmsman of his crew. An answer of 'yes' is unlikely to serve any useful purpose.

Written evidence may be accepted at the discretion of the protest committee, but of course there will need to be a very good reason why the witness cannot be present. The written evidence must be made available to the other side, or to both sides when it comes from a third party. Protest committees will naturally be alert to the disadvantages of not having the witness available for questioning.

Photographic evidence (still and video) is often offered: parties and committees should be wary, and Appendix P warns of its ambiguous nature.

Normally when a statement is made by one party and not refuted or questioned by the other it may be accepted as fact, but if, for instance, one party has failed to turn up, the protest committee should ask all the questions necessary before proceeding to a decision (rule 63.3(b)).

When a member of the protest committee has seen an incident and wishes to give evidence he may do so, but only in the presence of the parties. All questions must be asked then, and the parties *must* feel secure that the witness's privileged position will not result in him giving more information in their absence. Rule Q3.2 states: 'When it is considered desirable that some members not participate in discussing and deciding a protest, the jury remains properly constituted if at least three members remain.' It is important to make sure that neither of the parties feels aggrieved.

Finding facts The evidence has been given and the protest committee *must* now 'find the facts and base its decision on them', and the better the evidence, the easier it will be to find these sometimes elusive facts.

What is a fact? A protest committee must keep facts and interpretations separate. The protestor (S) makes a statement that she bore away and passed 6 feet astern of P; P states that S did not bear away, and passed 15 feet astern of her. These are two contradictory statements. After questioning parties and witnesses, the jury comes to the following conclusions: that S did bear away; that S passed 6 feet astern of P; and that there is doubt as to whether P could have crossed without collision had S not borne away. These are the facts found by the jury; these are the facts that cannot be changed by an appeal authority (rule 70.1).

As the story unfolds, make mental notes of the facts you will have to arrive at and the questions you need to ask to get the evidence for arriving satisfactorily at those facts. When the jury is alone, make sure that you find the facts before proceeding to interpret them. Only now, with the facts determined, will the jury turn to the interpretation of the applicable rule, with the help of any available case law. Given those facts, did P infringe rule 10? The jury will interpret the rule in the light of the facts it has already found; an interpretation that may be changed on appeal.

The line between facts and interpretation is sometimes very difficult to draw; for example, to say that L gave W room to keep clear is not a fact. The facts might be that L established an overlap three minutes before the incident, that it was established 10 feet to leeward, and that W had no obstruction to windward of her. These facts can then be interpreted to say that L gave W room to keep clear.

ISAF 58 makes an important point. Decisions must be made on facts, not on intent. A boat that luffed with every intention of tacking, but never went beyond head to wind, was held not to have broken rule 13. However, in rules 2 and 69 intent will have to be considered: a man spills beer over the chairman of the jury: he did it in a temper – gross misconduct; he did it by mistake – he did nothing wrong; he was putting out a fire from a pipe in the chairman's pocket – he deserves a medal! Thus can circumstances alter cases.

Rule 63.7 Protests Between Boats in Different Races
This is a rare occurrence, but one that can cause ill-feeling if not resolved with tact.

Rule 64 Protest Decisions

64.1   Penalties and Exoneration

(a) When the protest committee decides that a boat that is a *party* to the hearing has broken a *rule*, she shall be disqualified unless some other penalty applies. A penalty shall be imposed whether or not the applicable *rule* was mentioned in the *protest*.

(b) When as a consequence of breaking a *rule* a boat has compelled another boat to break a *rule*, rule 64.1(a) does not apply to the other boat and she shall be exonerated.

(c) If a boat has broken a *rule* when not *racing*, her penalty shall apply to the race sailed nearest in time to that of the incident.

64.2   Decisions on Redress

When the protest committee decides that a boat is entitled to redress under rule 62, it shall make as fair an arrangement as possible for all boats affected, whether or not they asked for redress. This may be to adjust the scoring (see rule A4 for some examples) or finishing times of boats, to *abandon* the race, to let the results stand or to make some other arrangement. When in doubt about the facts or probable results of any arrangement for the race or series, especially before *abandoning* the race, the protest committee shall take evidence from appropriate sources.

64.3 Decisions on Measurement Protests

(a) When the protest committee finds that deviations in excess of tolerances specified in the class rules were caused by damage or normal wear and do not improve the performance of the boat, it shall not penalize her. However, the boat shall not *race* again until the deviations have been corrected, except when the protest committee decides there is or has been no reasonable opportunity to do so.

(b) When the protest committee is in doubt about the meaning of a measurement rule, it shall refer its questions, together with the relevant facts, to an authority responsible for interpreting the rule. In making its decision, the committee shall be bound by the reply of the authority.

(c) When a boat disqualified under a measurement rule states in writing that she intends to appeal, she may compete in subsequent races without changes to the boat, but will be disqualified if she fails to appeal or the appeal is decided against her.

(d) Measurement costs arising from a *protest* involving a measurement rule shall be paid by the unsuccessful *party* unless the protest committee decides otherwise.

Rule 64.1 Penalties and Exoneration

The authority of all protest committees to disqualify or otherwise penalize a boat stems from this rule, except umpiring in Appendices C and D, and doping and advertising infringements under Appendices G and L, which include their own arrangements.

Disqualification under rule 64.1 can only follow a decision by a protest committee that a boat has broken a rule, although there are exceptions to this discussed in rule 63.1, and sailing instructions can change the penalties. The rule is mandatory: if a boat breaks a rule the protest committee must disqualify her unless rule 64.1(b) applies. The exception (and is there a rule in the book that does *not* have an exception?) is rule H4, which permits the protest committee to give a warning about wrong sail numbers or letters.

Rule 64.1(b) makes it clear that you may sometimes be forced to break a rule and therefore you should not be punished. In ISAF 19 (Fig 51), P tried and failed to cross ahead of M. M tacked to avoid her, hailing as she did so. S tried to respond, but there was contact. P retired. S protested M under rule 10 and the protest committee, commenting that M had

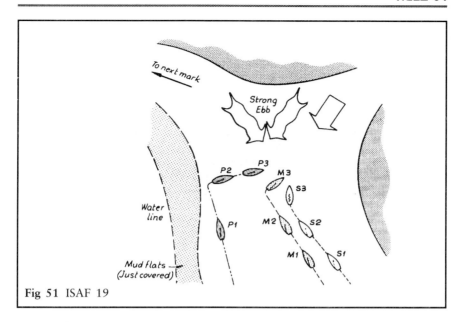

Fig 51 ISAF 19

had sufficient time to take avoiding action to keep clear of both P and S, disqualified M under rule 14. M appealed successfully, with the RYA saying: 'P, which properly retired, infringed rule 10. She caused the problem and M, in the circumstances, took proper action to reduce the effects of P's error of judgement. Both M and S were the innocent victims of P's failure to observe the rules, M is reinstated, and S is not to be penalized. Rule 14 was not broken.' It is interesting to notice here that, whatever the rules were then, today rule 19 would not be applicable (see under the definition Obstruction). ISAF 114, RYA 89/12, ISAF 114, US 71, US 116 and US 139 also illustrate this point.

The fact that the relevant rule number, say 10, has not been mentioned anywhere on the protest form or during the hearing need not deter the protest committee from penalizing a boat that, it decides, has broken that rule. In US 186 (a case looked at under rule 16), two boats protested each other under rules 11, 15 and 17, but the decision was firmly based on rule 16. This marks a big departure from the law, where, if you have not been charged under section 1 you cannot be found guilty of breaking section 1. At first sight the freedom to use any rule might seem unfair, but if it were not so, every Part 2 protest would simply quote every rule of Part 2 and that would get no one anywhere. When the committee's decision is properly based on the facts disclosed by the evidence at the hearing the subject matter of the relevant rule must have been discussed.

Rule 64.2 Decisions on Redress

The criteria for getting redress are in rule 62, and that rule and this one should be studied together.

First, the following decision must be reached: is the boat eligible or not? Sometimes it is obvious that one boat has spent a long time helping another; at other times, much evidence will be needed. Time is occasionally wasted, as when the self-esteem of a race officer will not permit him to admit a mistake, or, after redress has been decided and the hearing is over, a dozen boats come forward with quite a different story, all seeking redress in their turn.

Once decided that a boat is eligible for redress, the protest committee can start examining the evidence to make sure that it has spread its net wide enough for witnesses, or indeed for parties. It is essential to hear enough evidence to get a good overall picture, and sometimes the best way to do that is to make the whole fleet a party to the hearing, and hear them all, with the race officer. I have been present on three occasions when the whole fleet was invited, and in each case it has led to all the facts being quickly made clear, and to a fairer decision than would otherwise have been possible. In addition, justice is seen to be done; there is nothing hidden; everybody can be questioned.

The protest committee has a duty of fairness not only to the boat seeking redress, but also to the whole fleet, and it must 'make as fair an arrangement as possible for all boats affected'. The most drastic action is to abandon the race, a course that is to be avoided whenever possible. There are often appeals where several boats have sailed the correct course and finished, only to have the race abandoned because another two had been prejudiced because of a race officer's mistake. In such cases, the appeals committees often uphold the appeal, order the race to be reinstated, and suggest suitable redress for those who suffered from the mistake.

Suitable redress is fairly easy when the incident occurs at or near the finishing line, but it is almost impossible when there is a mistake at the start. An error in the starting procedure that affects one or more boats, and is allowed to stand without there being a postponement or a general recall, ruins the race. Like Humpty Dumpty, it cannot be put together again. If the race is abandoned, those who won will object; if places are given (or time), the prejudiced boats will claim to have been placed too low, the rest will maintain that the new placings are unjustifiably generous; if average points are awarded to a good calm-weather boat, others will say it was a day of high winds when she would have done badly. However, there is no getting out of it – the jury is compelled to play 'God' and do as best it can.

118

One thing a jury must not do is to put boats that have made a mistake ahead of those that have not. ISAF 102, where a race committee tried to set a finish contrary to the definition, states: 'If the protest committee is satisfied that the course ordered was such that some boats were prejudiced, so as to alter the results of the race, it is open to the committee to award points to such boats, but it would not be equitable for such boats to rank higher than those that finished correctly.'

US 243 makes the important point that correcting an incorrect score is not prejudicial to a boat's finishing position; not correcting it prejudices the other competitors.

Rule 64.3 Decisions on Measurement Protests

See also rule 78, Compliance with Class Rules; Certificates.

I dread measurement protests where things seem never to be black or white, always a muddy grey. At a major event, competitors or their coaches will have the necessary class rules, but make sure if you are chairing the jury that you yourself have a copy. The protest will be as normal, a hearing with the parties and their witnesses – probably 'expert' witnesses such as measurers and class officials.

Rule 64.3(a) starts with a let-out clause – a means whereby a boat that does not measure can get away with it, but only to a very limited extent. When frequent use or damage has caused measurements to go beyond the tolerances written into the class rules, a boat need not be penalized; however, she must put it right as soon as possible.

And while on the subject of tolerances, remember that they are only that. There cannot be a tolerance of a tolerance. If the permitted thickness is 20–25 mm with a tolerance of 2 mm, anything smaller than 18 mm or bigger than 27 mm is out of class. The fact that all the competitors have skilfully improved their boat to 25 mm and then some go beyond 27 mm is just tough.

Rule 64.3(b) requires a protest committee to decide a measurement protest in the same way as any other, provided it has no doubt. That the sail is a metre too long on the foot is easily dealt with immediately, but where the black band is alleged to be 3 centimetres too far out and it is a question of how you measure the position of that band, then there is doubt, and the protest committee must ask for expert advice. It must 'refer its questions, together with the relevant facts, to an authority responsible for interpreting the rule'. It is not always easy to determine who this authority may be. Sometimes designated by class rules, this authority will usually be the chief class measurer. It is wise to know the identity and whereabouts of this person before an important series starts so that any problem can be dealt with as quickly as possible. US 226 confirms that the protest committee is bound by the authority's reply.

Rule 65 Informing the Parties and Others

65.1 After making its decision, the protest committee shall promptly inform the *parties* to the hearing of the facts found, the applicable *rules*, the decision, the reasons for it, and any penalties imposed or redress given.

65.2 A *party* to the hearing is entitled to receive the above information in writing, provided she asks for it in writing from the protest committee within seven days of being informed of the decision. The committee shall then promptly provide the information, including, when relevant, a diagram of the incident prepared or endorsed by the committee.

65.3 When the protest committee penalizes a boat under a measurement rule, it shall send the above information to the relevant measurement authorities.

All plain sailing here: the job done, it only remains to tell the parties what you have decided and give it to them in writing if they want it. Most losers merely want to forget they have lost and get on with the next thing, but sometimes a angry protestee has every intention of getting the decision upset in appeal. In such cases, even if there is no time to write out a detailed version of the case, make sure you have enough notes to be able to put it together afterwards.

Every chairman will have his own views, but my recommendation is to explain rule interpretations when asked to do so, or in a teaching situation with children etc, but be careful not to go into the reasons why you have believed X rather than Y. If you do, you may find yourself in deep trouble!

You may also meet the sailor who, having lost, threatens an appeal, thinking that this will make you look at your decision again and alter your views. Well, you may or may not, but a word of welcome such as 'How interesting' often takes the wind out of his sails and no appeal follows.

Rule 66 Reopening a Hearing

> The protest committee may reopen a hearing when it decides that it may have made a significant error, or when significant new evidence becomes available within a reasonable time. It shall reopen a hearing when required by the national authority under rule F5. A *party* to the hearing may ask for a reopening no later than 24 hours after being informed of the decision. When a hearing is reopened, a majority of the members of the protest committee shall, if possible, be members of the original protest committee.

Requests for reopening are fairly common. Only parties to the hearing can ask for a reopening; this needs to be strictly adhered to, otherwise the whole fleet would be asking for one. The time limit for the request is 24 hours, but the hearing may be later if, say, a French video cannot immediately be shown on a British television set and time is needed to sort this out. Usually a jury is only too eager to get significant new evidence, since the hearing has often produced a jumble of dubious, contradictory facts from which it has had to erect a plausible story whereby to penalize one of the boats. Now, perhaps (though, alas, rarely), with new evidence, all will be revealed. The jury look at the film or hear the witness (at this stage there is no need to have both parties present) and then decide if the new evidence confirms the previous decision, throws no new light on the incident, or shows something unexpected that may indeed change the outcome. Only in the last instance will all the parties be summoned and the case formally reopened.

Do not be afraid to admit that you may have been wrong. The competitors may think you indecisive, but usually they will be glad that someone is giving so much time and thought to their special case.

Rule 67 Rule 42 and Hearing Requirement

> When so stated in the sailing instructions, the protest committee may penalize without a hearing a boat that has broken rule 42, provided that a member of the committee or its designated observer has seen the incident. A boat so penalized shall be informed by notification in the race results.

Rule 67 refers only to events where a jury (international or not) is present and some members of it at sea. A form of this rule is often used in championship events, where, warned by a yellow flag, competitors can do a turn at the first offence, get disqualified for the second, and are out of the regatta for the third. Firm-minded judges who are conversant with the class can, by use of the yellow flag in the practice race or the first race, virtually ensure that rule 42 is not broken any further during the event.

There is no proviso for a competitor to get a hearing on request, but this is one of the occasions when he could ask for redress for an improper action of the protest committee under rule 62.1(a).

68 Damages

> The question of damages arising from a breach of any *rule* shall be governed by the prescriptions, if any, of the national authority.

Section C – Gross Misconduct

Rule 69 Allegations of Gross Misconduct

69.1 Action by a Protest Committee

(a) When a protest committee, from its own observation or a report received, believes that a competitor may have committed a gross breach of a *rule* or of good manners or sportsmanship, or may have brought the sport into disrepute, it may call a hearing. The protest committee shall promptly inform the competitor in writing of the alleged misconduct and of the time and place of the hearing.

(b) A protest committee of at least three members shall conduct the hearing, following rules 63.2, 63.3, 63.4 and 63.6. If it decides that the competitor committed the alleged misconduct it shall either

    (1) warn the competitor or
    (2) impose a penalty by excluding the competitor, and a boat, when appropriate, from a race, or the remaining races of a series or the entire series, or by taking other action within its jurisdiction.

(c) The protest committee shall promptly report a penalty, but not a warning, to the national authorities of the venue, of the competitor and of the boat owner.

(d) If the competitor has left the venue and cannot be notified or fails to attend the hearing, the protest committee shall collect all available evidence and, when the allegation seems justified, make a report to the relevant national authorities.

(e) When the protest committee has left the event and a report alleging misconduct is received, the race committee or organizing authority may appoint a new protest committee to proceed under this rule.

69.2 Action by a National Authority

(a) When a national authority receives a report required in rule 69.1(c) or rule 69.1(d), or a report alleging a gross breach of a *rule* or of good manners or sportsmanship or conduct that brought the sport into disrepute, it may conduct an investigation and, when appropriate, shall conduct a hearing. It may then take any disciplinary action within its jurisdiction it considers appropriate against the competitor or boat, or other person involved, including suspending eligibility, permanently or for a specified period of time, to compete in any event held within its jurisdiction, and suspending ISAF eligibility under rule K3.1(a).

(b) The national authority of a competitor shall also suspend the ISAF eligibility of the competitor as required in rule K3.1(a).

(c) The national authority shall promptly report a suspension of eligibility under rule 69.2(a) to the ISAF, and to the national authorities of the person or the owner of the boat suspended if they are not members of the suspending national authority.

69.3 Action by the ISAF
Upon receipt of a report required by rules 69.2(c) and K4.1, the ISAF shall inform all national authorities, which may also suspend eligibility for events held within their jurisdiction. The ISAF Executive Committee shall suspend the competitor's ISAF eligibility as required in rule K3.1(a) if the competitor's national authority does not do so.

Rule 69 is not an ordinary rule, it is not a protest and, looking back at rule 60.1, it is clear that it cannot be invoked by a boat or a competitor; to repeat, one boat cannot protest another under this rule; and a competitor can only put in a report to the protest committee and hope that the protest committee will act on it. The protest committee may act on anybody's report – an interested party's, a competitor's, or a report from the race committee as well as on its own observation (for example, a protest committee would obviously look carefully at any disqualification under rule 2). Note that the verb is always 'may'. The protest committee is presented with a report, but it need not act if it does not think fit. I would not expect a jury to take more than ten minutes to decide if they want to open a hearing or not. I heard of a preliminary hearing, which took two months to arrange, held merely to decide whether or not to open a hearing. This must be the wrong way to go and will, I hope, never be repeated.

There is no time limit for initiating a '69', though with the passage of time, collecting reliable evidence becomes more difficult.

While the report can be oral, the protest committee must issue a written allegation (similar to a protest). I suggest something simple:

> The XYZ World Championship 24 June 1998
> To: James Doe
> From: The International Jury
> Subject: Rule 69 Hearing
>> You are requested to appear before the Jury at 1930 on 25 June 1998 for a hearing under rule 69 to investigate an incident during the fourth race at the first windward mark in which it is alleged that you deliberately capsized GBR 123 by holding her gunwhale under the water.
> John Justice, Chairman, International Jury

The hearing will be as if it were a protest, subject to the same protections for the 'accused'. By their very nature, '69' cases are delicate; they reflect on the competitor's character because he has acted with intent. It is this intent that differentiates them from other actions. They often deal with unpleasant matters: cheating, dishonesty, foul language, loutishness, drunkenness, etc, and a wrong decision could be libellous. Publication might be privileged, but could lead to a court action, costly even if the competitor is unsuccessful. For this reason, the protest committee should stick rigidly to the letter of the rules, but within reason give any benefit of doubt to the 'accused': give him more time, wait for his witnesses, let him have his lawyer present (though you may forbid the latter to speak), and generally make sure he has no grounds for procedural complaint. Keep very detailed notes of everything that is said and done.

Views differ as to the scope of this rule; a gross breach of a rule or of good sportsmanship is almost certainly linked to the race or to another competitor; a gross breach of good manners may reach further and be more difficult to identify. Help comes from the phrase 'may have brought the sport into disrepute'. A committee will not act under rule 69 when a competitor beats his wife (unless perhaps she is his crew!) or defrauds his company, for the action is clearly not connected to the sport of sailing. The rule is properly invoked when a competitor *during* a regatta or series, *at* the site of the event (host club, marina, race area, town hall reception), conducts himself (or herself) improperly towards someone who is connected with the event (organizers and race committee, marina staff, party hosts, spectators, press and, of course, fellow competitors and their families). The good name of the sport must be protected. The unstinting volunteer helpers on whom all events rely, the sponsors who make some events possible, the host clubs that make visitors so welcome – all will be unwilling to play their essential parts if a firm stand is not taken against misbehaviour. No rules can be laid down; each sad case is unique.

When the misdeed has been proved, the protest committee has two possibilities: first, it may warn. This is not a penalty and need not be reported to the national authority. It is a useful weapon because, fortunately, a heartfelt apology and a dressing-down is often all that is needed. Secondly, the protest committee may penalize, but of course its powers are limited, the maximum being to throw the competitor out of the whole regatta. When it penalizes, it must report the incident to the national authority.

Because misbehaviour sometimes mars the prize-giving (a long period of waiting with the bar open is too tempting), the two final paragraphs, (d) and (e), of rule 69.1 suggest ways of dealing with the absence of the competitor or the jury.

The following list gives the subject matter of the few published cases. It is clear that the last race of a top championship brings temptations, but the introduction of giving redress to the victims of such skulduggery has certainly improved things.

ISAF 78:   OCS does not return and harasses another boat. OCS is disqualified from whole series.
ISAF 135:   Similar to ISAF 78 after infringing black flag rule.
ISAF 137:   Boat in race deliberately collides with one not racing and commits gross breach of the rules.
CYA 102:   Competitor demands with obscenities that mark be moved, then moves it himself. Gross breach of good manners and sportsmanship.
RYA 86/6:   A boat abandoned a race and then hindered another. Breach of good sportsmanship.

Rule 69.2 takes matters into the hands of the national authority, which can act on any report from anyone, but while a protest committee has held a hearing and heard the evidence, other reports may necessitate a hearing by the national authority itself.

Under rule 69.3, when the national authority has dealt with the competitor, the ISAF may confirm or increase the penalty and the competitor will very likely come under the restrictions outlined in Appendix K, Competitors' ISAF Eligibility.

Section D – Appeals

Rule 70 Right of Appeal and Requests for Interpretations

70.1 Provided that the right of appeal has not been denied under rule 70.4, a protest committee's interpretation of a *rule* or its procedures, but not the facts in its decision, may be appealed to the national authority of the venue by

(a) a boat or competitor that is a *party* to a hearing, or

(b) a race committee that is a *party* to a hearing, provided the protest committee is a jury.

70.2 A protest committee may request confirmation or correction of its decision.

70.3 A club or other organization affiliated to a national authority may request an interpretation of the *rules*, provided no *protest* that may be appealed is involved.

70.4 There shall be no appeal from the decisions of an international jury constituted in compliance with Appendix Q. Furthermore, if the notice of race and the sailing instructions so state, the right of appeal may be denied provided that

(a) it is essential to determine promptly the result of a race that will qualify a boat to compete in a later stage of an event or a subsequent event (a national authority may prescribe that its approval is required for such a procedure),

(b) a national authority so approves for a particular event open only to entrants under its own jurisdiction, or

(c) a national authority after consultation with the ISAF so approves for a particular event, provided the jury is constituted as required by Appendix Q, except that only two members of the jury need be International Judges.

70.5 Appeals and requests shall conform to Appendix F.

The most useful long-term work of an appeals committee is probably to ensure that there is consistency in the decisions and judgements of the protest committees throughout its area. If there were no RYA appeals authority, it would be easy to conceive of a protest committee in Cowes interpreting the rules in a different way from one at Grafham

Water; or perhaps the Dragon class would sail to a slightly different interpretation of rule 16 than the Lasers. This would make it difficult for helmsmen to change areas or swap classes. The ISAF, by its November meetings and its book *Interpretations of the Racing Rules*, strives continuously to arrive at international consistency, so that at world championships or the Olympic Games, helmsmen from all over the world play the same game. In the last 16 years there has been a great improvement thanks to the appointment of nearly 400 International Judges and, more recently, of International Umpires and International Race Managers. Regular seminars are held for the interchange of ideas, and every effort will be made in the next four years to achieve equally good consistency using the new rules.

Appeals based on new or difficult interpretations are always welcome, while appeals on facts are not allowed (rule 70.1). If the protest committee has not followed the requirements of Part 5 for a fair and valid hearing, an appeal committee cannot reverse the findings of fact, or find facts itself; it can only send the case back for a re-hearing. After hearing all the evidence, when the protest committee states that L was 6 feet from W, an appeals committee will not – indeed, is not permitted to – change that figure to 10 feet. It has no knowledge on which to base such a change. However, the interpretation of that distance, as to whether 6 feet was or was not 'room', belongs in the province of the appeals committee.

The number of those who can go to appeal is limited to a party to the hearing: a boat, a competitor (rarely), or a race committee when there has been a jury. It is important to stress this. When *Buttercup* asks for and gets redress, *Daisy* cannot appeal. She is not a party to the hearing and she must ask for redress in her turn. Her request will be heard, and then, if she does not like the outcome, she may appeal. If this were not so, the appeals committee would have no facts from the protest committee to interpret.

Rule 70.4 lays down the instances when there is no appeal. First, there is none from the decisions of a properly constituted international jury. If, for some reason, the jury is not in accordance with Appendix Q, its decisions will be open to appeal. In RYA 83/4, the organizing authority meant to appoint an international jury, but only four members appeared, so that the jury was never adequately constituted. It followed that the competitors had the right of appeal, and that the appeal was duly accepted, heard and then dismissed! The organizing authority need not give notice of an international jury, but a sensible race committee will publish a list of the jury members in the sailing instructions or on the official notice board.

In contrast, when there is to be no appeal because final results are needed immediately in order to continue the competition (and there is no international jury), it must be notified in both the notice of race and the sailing instructions, and is only allowed in the three limited circumstances stated. A national authority can ask for approval in the first of these three (as does the RYA), as it is a serious matter to deprive competitors of their right of appeal.

Rule 71 Appeal Decisions

71.1 No *interested party* or member of the protest committee shall take any part in the discussion or decision on an appeal or a request for confirmation or correction.

71.2 The national authority may uphold, change or reverse a protest committee's decision, declare the *protest* invalid, or return the *protest* for a new hearing and decision by the same or a different protest committee.

71.3 When from the facts found by the protest committee the national authority decides that a boat that was a *party* to the hearing broke a *rule*, it shall penalize her, whether or not that boat or that *rule* was mentioned in the protest committee's decision.

71.4 The decision of the national authority shall be final. The national authority shall send its decision in writing to all *parties* to the hearing and the protest committee, who shall be bound by the decision.

There is no need for me to address appeals committees. Their members will be experienced in the rules and used to judging. In the RYA, where I have had the honour to chair the appeals committee for many years, we invite each of our UK International Judges to sit on the committee for a year. This has proved a very good move, for it has given the committee the chance to know the judges and the judges a picture of life on the other side. Organizing authorities and race committees cannot use sailing instructions to protect themselves against appeal decisions. Results, prizes and cups must follow any appeal decision, however much it upsets their plans (ISAF 131).

(Numbers 72–74 are spare numbers)

Part 6 – Entry and Qualification

Rule 75 Entering a Race

75.1 To enter a race, a boat shall comply with the requirements of the organizing authority of the race. She shall be entered by

(a) a member of a club or other organization affiliated to a national authority,

(b) such a club or organization, or

(c) a member of a national authority.

75.2 Competitors shall comply with Appendix K, if applicable.

For a boat to race she must be entered by someone or some organization that falls within the framework of this rule. There is a link between the ISAF and the person entering the boat. *Daisy*'s owner is a member of the club, the club is affiliated to the national authority, the national authority to the ISAF, and so the chain is complete. There are variations on the theme, but the link should always be there. For example, if the town regatta is organized by the town committee and the town sailing club, the latter being affiliated to the national authority, the regatta is legitimate. If the regatta is run by the town committee alone, no great harm is done, but there is no right of appeal.

This is a good place to look at entry forms. Rule M1.2(4) brings the organizing authority's attention to the necessity for an entry form. The form will ask for such mundane information as names, addresses, phone, fax and e-mail numbers, the boat's name, sail number, hull colour etc; more importantly, the owner should sign a declaration that he will be bound by the rules. Ignorance of the law is no excuse, for the signatory is presumed to have read and understood all the rules, just as when driving a car we are presumed to know the *Highway Code*.

Each entry form is adapted to the individual requirements of the event and may need such information as nationality, sex or age. Almost certainly the form will carry a warning that a late entry will be refused or cost a large additional fee. The inability of competitors to make timely entries remains a wonder for experienced race organizers.

Rule 76 Exclusion of Boats or Competitors

76.1 The organizing authority or the race committee may reject or cancel the entry of a boat or exclude a competitor, subject to rule 76.2, provided it does so before the start of the first race and states the reason for doing so.

76.2 At world and continental championships no entry within stated quotas shall be rejected or cancelled without first obtaining the approval of the relevant international class association (or the Offshore Racing Council) or the ISAF.

A competitor has no absolute right to enter a race. The organizing authority or the race committee can refuse him entry, but it must give a reason. I take it that the reason need not be very detailed. A phrase such as 'After the incident last Saturday, you will realize that the Club has no other option but to refuse your entry' will probably suffice, provided that there has in fact been an incident. In US 267, the race committee thought that a boat, while not offending against any safety regulations, was not seaworthy enough for a long race and rejected the entry. The boat asked for redress, saying that the action of the race committee was discriminatory and that there should be a legitimate reason. The protest committee supported the race committee and she appealed. Dismissing the appeal it was said: 'The appellant's belief that the rule requires a "legitimate" reason is incorrect, because rule 76 does not impose qualitative tests for the reason. In the absence of such tests, a race committee has broad authority to make such judgements as it considers necessary to ensure that a race is conducted in accordance with the intentions of the organizing authority as well as with the rules.'

Rule 77 Identification on Sails

A boat shall comply with the requirements of Appendix H governing class insignia, national letters and numbers on sails.

An unidentified boat might just as well not be in a race: she cannot be recalled at the start, she cannot be listed in the results, she cannot be protested; recognition is essential.

Sail insignia, letters and numbers are dealt with in Appendix H – an appendix that is always in force and that can be altered by national authority prescription and sailing instructions, but not by class rules except as permitted in the appendix itself.

Rule H4 gives a protest committee discretion to disqualify when the breach of the rules is blatant, or to warn when dealing with bad luck (perhaps a sail number torn off while racing). The discretionary power is there to help those in trouble with a minor point that does not affect the speed of the boat.

In RYA 81/12, a Fireball used a spinnaker with no number on it. The appeal decision, upholding her disqualification, stated that it was the owner's responsibility to maintain his boat in the condition upon which her certificate was based, including the requirement to carry the correct numbers on her sails. When the certificate was knowingly invalidated, rule 77 and the rules of Appendix H led to disqualification. Infringements of these rules are normally pursued only at championship level, events frequented by highly experienced crews who know (or should know) their class rules back to front and who will be expecting the rules to be administered rigidly.

Rule 78 Compliance with Class Rules; Certificates

78.1 A boat's owner and any other person in charge shall ensure that the boat is maintained to comply with her class rules and that her measurement or rating certificate, if any, remains valid.

78.2 When a *rule* requires a certificate to be produced before a boat *races*, and it is not produced, the boat may *race* provided that the race committee receives a statement signed by the person in charge that the valid certificate exists and that it will be given to the race committee before the end of the event. If the certificate is not received in time, the boat's scores shall be removed from the event results.

78.3 When a measurer for an event concludes that a boat does not comply with her class rules, he shall report the matter in writing to the race committee, which shall protest the boat.

It is the owner who is responsible for his boat being in class, although he may share that responsibility with the person in charge; it is obvious that when a company is the owner, an individual needs to be responsible too. There have been instances of 'cheating' boats being built, with some built-in advantage in size, in weight or with a forbidden fixture. If the boat is sold 'in class', it will be the owner who is liable. On the other hand, if the owner does not sail in a race and his skipper uses a too-large spinnaker, it is the skipper who will catch it. However, cheating apart, there are lots of people sailing around with no idea if their boat complies with her certificate or not, and not caring either:

'I bought an XOD 15 years ago and have a valid certificate, what else can I do?' Well, read the latest class rules, see what has changed in those 15 years, check with your class measurer, and make sure you are not caught out.

It has been said that measurement protests are no different from any other, but they are often charged with emotion because they tend to imply cheating rather than an innocent mistake, and are difficult because we have little experience of them. Case law is scarce; most of the bitterly fought cases happen at international meetings with an international jury and no appeal. A measurement protest may arise from a simple misunderstanding about the interpretation or application of an unclear rule (or even a clear one). It is easy to understand why cheating so often comes to mind: when an owner goes to the limit of, or beyond, a class rule it is always because of an item that makes *Daisy* faster, never slower. It is a rule that needs to be very strictly applied; there is no point in racing at all if the boats are not in class or not handicapped as they should be. The boat with an unfair advantage might just as well pull out a pair of oars and row. However, RYA 89/13, dealing with a spray hood suspected as serving as a sail, holds that standard equipment in a normal position does not invalidate a boat's certificate.

It is doubtful whether *Daisy* can be protested for simply being 'too fast'. On the face of it, the protest should allege some specific point that constitutes the infringement – for example, that the propeller installation has been altered contrary to the class rules or that the rudder is bigger than it should be. But there may be occasions when the protestor *cannot* suggest a reason and yet may *know* that *Daisy* was sailing faster than her rating or her class warrants. In this case, *Daisy* may be remeasured, and, if found to be in class, the protestor will pay for the remeasurement.

After how long can a boat discovered not to measure, be disqualified retrospectively? If cheating can be proved, then the answer is probably as far back as anyone wants – to last year's race perhaps, or even to three years ago. But the probability of producing adequate evidence gets very remote. Otherwise, lacking any evidence of cheating, it will be too late when a series, prize-giving and all, is over. ISAF 123 states: 'An in-date, authorized certificate, presented in good faith by an owner who has complied with the requirements of rule 78.1, cannot be retrospectively invalidated after a race or series is completed.'

See also rule 64.3, Decisions on Measurement Protests.

Rule 79 Advertising

> A boat and her crew shall comply with Appendix G.

A definition of advertising is given at the beginning of Appendix G. There is only one case as far as I am aware. US 279 lays it down that 'sail bags and turtles' are equipment, and therefore subject to the limitations of rule G3.1(e).

Rule 80 Rescheduled Races

> When a race has been rescheduled, rule 36 applies and all boats entered in the original race shall be notified and, unless disqualified under rule 30.3, be entitled to sail the rescheduled race. New entries that meet the entry requirements of the original race may be accepted at the discretion of the race committee.

A race that has been abandoned can be rescheduled to another day or another week, and the race committee must make sure that the time and place for the new race are known to all concerned. Starters in the original race have a right to start in the resail, but if they infringed the Z flag rule (30.2) and the race is resailed because of a general recall, then they will carry the penalty through with them to the resailed race. If they have infringed the black flag rule (30.3), they will be prohibited from starting.

Sailing instructions can alter this rule and restrict entries to starters in the original race if so desired.

See also rule 36, Races to be Restarted or Resailed.

(Numbers 81–84 are spare numbers)

Part 7 – Race Organization

Part 7 is for organizing authorities and race committees. There is no rule in Part 7 that can be infringed, but it tells competitors what they may expect in a well-run series, or where an indifferent one has gone astray. The importance of having races organized on a proper basis needs emphasizing. If race organizers are to have maximum protection against lawsuits from disgruntled competitors, and if competitors are to enjoy the good racing they are entitled to expect, then the racing must be efficiently and correctly planned within a recognized framework, competently conducted and fairly judged.

Part 7 cannot be altered by national authorities, sailing instructions or class rules.

Rule 85 Governing Rules

> The organizing authority, race committee and protest committee shall be governed by the *rules* in the conduct and judging of races.

We saw in rule 3 that a competitor is bound by the rules; now we see that all those running the event are also bound by them. Furthermore, by stepping outside the rules they might lay themselves open to claims for redress, or possibly even to being sued. It is not only the racing rules and sailing instructions that govern organizers, race and protest committees, but also those rules called in by sailing instructions: class rules, championship rules, measurement rules, special regulations, rating rules, the notice of race, etc. There is good reason for this proliferation, but no wonder we all get a bit bewildered every now and again, particularly if we change the rules to suit our purposes.

Rule 86 Rule Changes

> **86.1** A racing rule may not be changed unless permitted in the rule itself or as follows:

(a) Prescriptions of a national authority may change a racing rule, but not the Definitions; a rule in the Introduction; Sportsmanship and the Rules; Part 1, 2 or 7; rule 43.1, 43.2, 69, 70, 71, 75, 76.2 or 79; a rule of an appendix that changes one of these rules; or Appendix G, J, K, L or Q.

(b) Sailing instructions may change a racing rule by referring specifically to it and stating the change, but not rule 76.1, Appendix F, or a rule listed in rule 86.1(a).

(c) Class rules may change only rules 42, 49, 50, 51, 52, 53 and 54.

86.2 If a national authority so prescribes, these restrictions do not apply if rules are changed to develop or test proposed rules in local races. The national authority may prescribe that its approval is required for such changes.

1 By a national authority Rule 86.1(a) lists the rules that a national authority cannot change by prescription, or anyhow else. They are rules that protect competitors' rights or lay down ISAF policy on such matters as advertising or drugs. The rules have never required a national authority to publish its prescriptions, but a competitor found to have transgressed a secret prescription would have a legitimate grouse against his national authority. Prescriptions are either printed under each rule prescribed to, or all together, with the rules asterisked.

2 By the race committee by sailing instructions Rule 86.1(b) prevents sailing instructions from altering the rules that a national authority cannot alter and adds two more. It also states that a racing rule may be changed only 'by referring specifically to it and stating the change'. This is extremely important. The racing rules may be altered only if the competitor is specifically warned.

In US 272, the race committee, in planning the scoring, tried to change a fundamental rule that could not be changed, and tried to change a rule that could be changed but made no specific reference to it. The result was that the sailing instructions were invalid, and as if they had not been written.

Specifying the rule changed can be done at the beginning:

'SI 19 (affecting RRS 27.1)', or, as Appendix N suggests, at the end, 'This changes rule 27.1'. Some sailing instructions print a helpful list of racing rules changed.

What is a change? I believe that *anything* is a change: making the rule stricter, less strict, or just slightly different. Not everyone agrees, but be on the safe side and make sure that rule 86.2(b) is complied with.

When sailing instructions change a racing rule correctly, the alteration will prevail, however undesirable. In FIV 69/13, sailing instructions altered rule 63.1 – the right to a hearing – permitting a jury to disqualify summarily. The Italian Appeals Committee said: 'This sailing instruction was pretty drastic and may be justly criticized. However, it does not alter any of the listed rules and therefore has the force of a rule. It follows that it must be respected by whoever has agreed to race. If a competitor does not wish to sail under such conditions he need only refuse invitations of this sort. If he accepts them he must abide by them.'

3 Class rules Rule 86.1(c) lists the few rules that can be altered by class associations: the propulsion rule, the rule governing crew position, and the group of rules at the end of Part 4 which are virtually class rules for handicap classes.

Can sailing instructions change class rules? We are not told, the answer being 'it depends'. Obviously sailing instructions for the Soling Worlds cannot change Soling Class Measurement Rules and allow a large spinnaker. Equally obviously, some changes in crew weight or crew number may be allowed in the CHS classes in the local town regatta. Rules M1.2(8) and M2.2(5) call for any changes to class rules to be in the notice of race and the sailing instructions, which should mean competitors who come from far away get no nasty surprises. RYA 81/12 states: 'Sailing instructions that purport to override measurement rules of an International Class either do not apply to a boat in that class or, when they do apply, [temporarily] invalidate her certificate.' And that goes for National classes as well. In ISAF 165, class rules stated that a protest flag was not necessary, but this was not repeated in sailing instructions and was therefore invalid. US 154 and US 228 uphold protest committee decisions that accorded with class rules.

Classes also often have Championship Rules, and a race committee may find it necessary to alter these, but this should only be done in consultation with the class association.

Rule 86.2 allows some testing in local races, described in US 278 as races in which normally the same group of people from a limited geographic area who regularly race together.

Rule 87 Organizing Authority; Notice of Race; Committee Appointments

87.1 Organizing Authority
Races shall be organized by an organizing authority, which shall be

(a) the ISAF;

(b) a member national authority of the ISAF;

(c) a club or other organization affiliated to a national authority;

(d) a class association, either with the approval of a national authority or in conjunction with an affiliated club; or

(e) an unaffiliated body in conjunction with an affiliated club.

87.2 Notice of Race; Committee Appointments
The organizing authority shall publish a notice of race that conforms to rule M1, appoint a race committee and, when appropriate, appoint a jury.

Rule 87.1 Organizing Authority

It is clear that an organizing authority, unless it is the national authority or the ISAF itself, must be linked to the ISAF through its national authority. Either the organizing authority itself is an affiliated body, or it will be working within an affiliated body. It was lack of a stable organizing authority, other than the New York Supreme Court, that used to wreak such havoc in the America's Cup. The organizing authority has three main jobs; it must:

1 appoint the race committee, perhaps a stalwart race officer on his own, or a carefully chosen, highly experienced group for a big international event;

2 appoint, when appropriate, a jury, international or not;

3 publish the notice of race.

87.2 Notice of Race; Committee Appointments

The notice of race may be a scribbled piece of paper on the club notice board, a message on a loud hailer, or a printed document widely circulated months before the event: the principle is the same. Rule M1 lists the necessary points.

It is not possible to alter a notice of race satisfactorily, simply because it is impossible to be sure that the alteration will reach all the original recipients, and for this reason the notice of race is not a defined rule or set of rules. When necessary, its provisions can be made rules by incorporating it into the sailing instructions, or individual paragraphs can be reprinted as sailing instructions. Many classes issue a provisional notice, sometimes in the yachting press, or their events are listed by the ISAF, and then a more detailed notice follows.

Rule 88 Race Committee; Sailing Instructions; Scoring

88.1 Race Committee
The race committee shall conduct races as directed by the organizing authority and as required by the *rules*.

88.2 Sailing Instructions

(a) The race committee shall publish written sailing instructions that conform to rule M2.

(b) The sailing instructions for an international event shall include, in English, the applicable prescriptions of the national authority.

(c) Changes to the sailing instructions shall be in writing and posted within the required time on the official notice board or, on the water, communicated to each boat before her warning signal. Oral changes may be given only on the water, and only if the procedure is stated in the sailing instructions.

88.3 Scoring
The race committee shall score a race or series as required in rule A1 and by the scoring system specified in the sailing instructions.

Rule 88.1 Race Committee

Often the race committee and the organizing authority are one and the same – the sailing committee of the club will act as both; on the other hand, occasionally the race committee will not be local and will fly in to do their job. In any case, the committee is governed by the rules and would be unwise to depart from them.

Who is the race committee? In the Introduction to the rules we are told that, '"Race committee" includes any person or committee performing a race committee function'. Thus it includes not only those specifically appointed by the organizing authority, but also anyone appointed by the race committee itself – the measurers, time-keepers, mark layers, and those hoisting flags and writing down results. Their mistakes will be mistakes of the race committee and, as such, subject to redress being given.

Although a race committee may, within reason, prescribe what it likes in the sailing instructions (provided it alters them correctly), it cannot adjust class rules or ignore sailing instructions when they happen to be inconvenient; 'a race committee is bound by the wording of its own sailing instructions, although its intentions were otherwise' – this is from an old case where the course displayed on the course board did not send the fleet where the race officer had wanted them to go.

There can be a grey area between the organizing authority and the race committee. Rule 62.1(a) only grants redress for misdeeds of the race committee (or protest committee), so if the organizing authority slips up, say in an event where it is providing the boats, it may be considered the responsibility of the organizing authority; thus a competitor whose boat is not in class will not be able to get redress. Given the widely varying situations, it seems improbable that the rule makers will ever be able to solve that problem entirely, and sailing instructions should make it clear what the position is.

Rule 88.2 Sailing Instructions

It is depressingly easy to write bad sailing instructions, and no experienced race officer would ever dare boast that he had never misled competitors, never been ambiguous, or never made a mistake. For this reason, before sailing instructions are printed, do not be too proud to ask for advice; in the UK, the RYA runs an advisory service, and I hope that other national authorities offer the same. Appendix M lists the points to be included, and Appendix N offers a guide to writing them which should be followed as far as possible. The fact that so many pages of the rules book is devoted to sailing instructions underlines their importance.

Consisting of a mixture of essential information for, and instruction to, competitors, good sailing instructions contribute greatly to the success of an event, while poor ones can spoil it.

Instructions to boats use the mandatory 'shall', intentions of the race committee use 'will', or, if the committee has some discretion, 'may'.

Here are the introductory principles from Appendix N on the writing of sailing instructions:

1 They should include only two types of statement: the intentions of the race committee and the obligations of competitors.

2 They should be concerned only with racing. Information about social events, assignment of moorings, etc, should be provided separately.

3 They should not change the racing rules except when clearly desirable.

4 They should not repeat or restate any of the racing rules.

139

5 They should not repeat themselves.

6 They should be in chronological order; that is, the order in which the competitor will use them.

7 They should, when possible, use words and phrases from the racing rules.

Now here are some of my own principles on the writing of sailing instructions:

8 They should be written simply, based on a clear idea. Legal language, however grand, will not clarify a muddled concept; it will only serve to hide it until some desperate competitor brings the ambiguity out in the open at a redress hearing.

9 They should be thoroughly revised every year; all too often, a visiting sailor gets caught out by the fact that sailing instructions have not kept pace with events. For example, a buoy is renamed and changed on the charts, but not in the instructions; hence *everyone* knows the old name, except the poor visitor!

10 They should not impose conditions that you will later not wish to enforce – for example, complicated requirements for lodging a valid protest. As far as possible, races should be won or lost on the water, not ashore.

11 They must be precise. In an RYA appeal, a hurriedly scribbled sailing instruction forbade boats to pass between the committee boat and the inner distance mark. Twenty minutes before the warning signal, a boat passed through and was disqualified. On appeal, she was reinstated. The buoy did not become a mark until the preparatory signal. Had the instruction used the term 'buoy', the race committee's intentions could have been fulfilled.

The course chalked up on the board on the committee boat is just as much a part of sailing instructions as the nicely printed pages with the club monogram on the front, and needs just as much thought, if not more. Accurately defining the course and the starting and finishing lines is the most important, and the most difficult, aspect of writing sailing instructions. Whenever possible, check the course you have set by tracing the course on a chart. Be very careful with looped marks. Looking at Fig 44 in rule 28, if the course loops a mark (and there may be good reasons for it doing so), it must be made absolutely clear that the mark is a rounding and not a boundary mark. Merely stating that the mark is to be passed may not establish its status as a rounding mark.

When doubt exists as to the interpretation of a sailing instruction it must be resolved in favour of the competitor (RYA 84/2). However, the competitors do not always have it their way, for US 179 holds that misinterpretation of sailing instructions when their meaning *is* clear does not mean they are ambiguous. Sailing instructions must be read carefully.

Rule 88.2(c) deals with the mechanics of changing sailing instructions. Ashore, all changes must be written. A change on the course board or on the club notice board may be adequate but where possible a copy of the change should be given to each boat. Sailing instructions must give a final time for changes, after which competitors can go afloat without worrying. Flag 'L' is the standard way of warning everyone that there is a change.

On the water, any change must be made before the warning signal and 'communicated' to each boat. This may consist of just the alteration of a course board, but it is perfectly possible to hand out a written note to every boat even in quite a big fleet. (I've done it!)

Oral instructions are allowed, but only when they have been detailed in the written sailing instructions and only on the water (but see rule B7). Giving magnetic courses by loud hailer is fine; but when there are no written instructions to that effect, the race officer can hail till he is blue in the face, yet any boat that does not hear, or hears but does not believe, will (if her finishing position is significantly worsened) be entitled to redress.

A number of cases confirm this. In RYA 82/7, a hail of 'general recall' was made on the loud-hailer and ignored by one boat. On appeal, it was held that she was entitled to disregard the shouted instructions because no such system was described in the sailing instructions, and the hail was therefore without effect. At first glance this might seem rather unfair, but on consideration it would not be right to expect a boat to obey unexpected, perhaps half audible, unofficial instructions.

ISAF 75 deals with similar problems.

Do not alter sailing instructions orally at briefings. If you *must* do this, make sure that a written instruction follows. I was once at a bilingual briefing where the instructions were different in each language. It was a miracle that no disaster followed. US 216 also points out the dangers of giving instructions at briefings.

Rule 88.3 Scoring

Appendix A is not included in either rule 86.1(a) or (b). I take it therefore that national authority prescriptions and sailing instructions are permitted to change rule A1, and that the requirement in this rule for race committees to score according to rule A1 means A1, or A1 legally amended. One form of scoring is not all that different from the next, and by and large the same boats will win whatever system is in use. What is certain is that the system used must be clear; it must cover all possibilities and it must not be ambiguous. Scoring, a very difficult subject, is discussed in Appendix A, which does its best to avoid the many pitfalls.

Rule 89 Protest Committee

A protest committee shall be

(a) a committee appointed by the race committee;

(b) a jury, which is separate from and independent of the race committee; or

(c) an international jury meeting the requirements of Appendix Q. A national authority may prescribe that its approval is required for the appointment of international juries for races within its jurisdiction, except those of the ISAF.

Rule 63.1 requires a protest committee to hear all protests; there are three types of such committees:

1 A committee appointed by the race committee; this may consist of race committee members themselves or other respected club members who devote their summer weekend evenings to this pastime.

2 A jury, which is separate from the race committee. No race committee member can sit on a jury, and a race committee can appeal a decision of a jury (rule 70.1(b)); apart from this, there is really very little difference technically between 1 and 2. However, for an important national event, the organizing authority is wise to set up a jury that is similar to an international jury, but that does not need foreign judges (who are expensive). There is much virtue in this because it gives a country the chance to train its judges for international events.

'A race committee may not alter or refuse to implement the decision of a jury' (ISAF 136). A jury referred a measurement matter to the Mirror class association and, as required by rule 64.3(b), accepted its report that some boats had broken class rules. The race committee thought the disqualification unfair and refused to alter the results. The class association appealed successfully.

3 An international jury; these august bodies are constituted by Appendix Q. Some national authorities, including the RYA, approve juries that operate within their jurisdiction. Very occasionally, advice is needed before the jury can be accepted, but in general this is merely done so that the national authority has some idea of what goes on.

Definitions

A term used as stated below is shown in italic type or, in preambles, in bold italic type.

Abandon A race that a race committee or protest committee *abandons* is void but may be resailed.

Clear Astern and Clear Ahead; Overlap One boat is *clear astern* of another when her hull and equipment in normal position are behind a line abeam from the aftermost point of the other boat's hull and equipment in normal position. The other boat is *clear ahead*. They *overlap* when neither is *clear astern* or when a boat between them *overlaps* both. These terms do not apply to boats on opposite *tacks* unless rule 18 applies.

Finish A boat *finishes* when any part of her hull, or crew or equipment in normal position, crosses the finishing line in the direction of the course from the last *mark* either for the first time or, if she takes a penalty, after complying with rule 31.2 or rule 44.2.

Interested Party A person who may gain or lose as a result of a protest committee's decision, or who has a close personal interest in the decision.

Keep Clear One boat *keeps clear* of another if the other can sail her course with no need to take avoiding action and, when the boats are *overlapped* on the same *tack*, if the *leeward* boat could change course without immediately making contact with the *windward* boat.

Leeward and Windward A boat's *leeward* side is the side that is or, when she is head to wind, was away from the wind. However, when sailing by the lee or directly downwind, her *leeward* side is the side on which her mainsail lies. The other side is her *windward* side. When two boats on the same *tack overlap*, the one on the *leeward* side of the other is the *leeward* boat. The other is the *windward* boat.

Mark An object the sailing instructions require a boat to pass on a specified side, excluding its anchor line and objects attached temporarily or accidentally.

Obstruction An object that a boat could not pass without changing course substantially, if she were sailing directly towards it and one of her hull lengths from it. An object that can be safely passed on only one side and an area so designated by the sailing instructions are also *obstructions*. However, a boat *racing* is not an *obstruction* to other boats unless they are required to *keep clear* of her or give her *room*.

Overlap See ***Clear Astern*** and ***Clear Ahead; Overlap***.

Party A *party* to a hearing: a protestor; a protestee; a boat requesting redress; any other boat or a competitor liable to be penalized, including under rule 69.1; a race commitee in a hearing under rule 62.1(a).

Postpone A *postponed* race is delayed before its scheduled start but may be started or *abandoned* later.

Proper Course A course a boat would sail to *finish* as soon as possible in the absence of the other boats referred to in the rule using the term. A boat has no *proper course* before her starting signal.

Protest An allegation by a boat, a race committee or a protest committee that a boat has broken a *rule*.

Racing A boat is *racing* from her preparatory signal until she *finishes* and clears the finishing line and *marks* or retires, or until the race committee signals a general recall, *postponement*, or *abandonment*.

Room The space a boat needs in the existing conditions while manoeuvring promptly in a seamanlike way.

Rule (a)   The rules in this book, including the Definitions, Race Signals, Introduction, preambles, and the rules of an appendix when it applies, but not titles;

(b)   the prescriptions of a national authority, when they apply;

(c)   the sailing instructions;

(d)   the class rules except any that conflict with the rules in this book;

(e)   any other documents governing the event.

Start A boat *starts* when after her starting signal any part of her hull, crew or equipment first crosses the starting line and she has complied with rule 29.1 and rule 30.1 if it applies.

Tack, Starboard or Port A boat is on the *tack, starboard* or *port,* corresponding to her *windward* side.

Two-Length Zone The area around a *mark* or *obstruction* within a distance of two hull lengths of the boat nearer to it.

Windward   See ***Leeward*** and ***Windward***.

Rule 86 forbids any changes to the 20 definitions – definitions of the most important terms found in the rules book, where a word is made to carry a wider and more exact meaning than it would have in ordinary use. Any national prescription or sailing instruction that purports to alter a definition will be automatically invalid. Whenever a word is used in its defined sense it is printed in italics.

Read the definitions very carefully – every word counts. When you come across 'keep clear', for instance, in the Part 2 rules, check that you know the exact meaning of the two words; do not rely on what may be a less than perfect recall of what the definition says.

Rule B1 has other definitions, *Capsized* and *Recovering*, for sailboard racing.

Abandon
(See Race Signals N, N over H and N over A, and rules 27.3 and 32.) A race that has been abandoned may be resailed sooner or later. Occasionally it may be resailed as the result of redress being given, but it is a heavy weapon to be employed as little as possible. Every effort must be made to resail an abandoned race.

Clear Astern *and* Clear Ahead; Overlap
When there are only two boats one must be clear astern or ahead of the other, or they must be overlapped; they cannot be both at the same time, for one precludes the other (Fig 52). As shown in Fig 53, a third boat alters the situation, and may or may not link the other two. Both boats must have their equipment in 'normal position'. That long sheet trailing astern of the boat outside you will not give you an overlap!

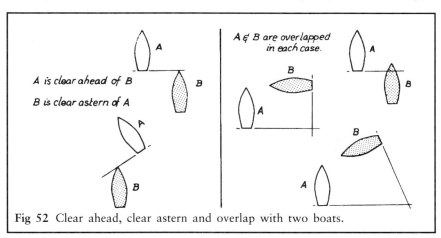

Fig 52 Clear ahead, clear astern and overlap with two boats.

ISAF 145 (Fig 29) shows clearly that the courses of two boats may differ by almost 180°, but they are still overlapped with all that that

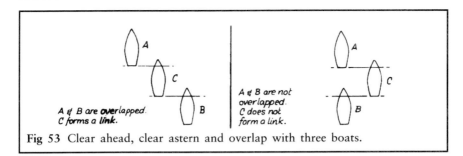

Fig 53 Clear ahead, clear astern and overlap with three boats.

implies. Circumstances will decide which of the two has right of way when overlapped.

Not surprisingly, there is an exception: the terms do not apply to opposite-tack boats except while passing marks.

Finish

Daisy usually finishes when she cuts the finishing line (it is always spoken of as 'crosses', but full crossing is not necessary – see rule 28.1) with any part of her hull, or her crew or equipment in normal position. The last qualification prevents an arm or a spinnaker pole being thrust forward to achieve an earlier finish.

There are occasions when she does not finish at that moment; she cuts the line and, before she has stopped 'racing', hits a mark. Now she must do a turn (on either side of the line) and cut the line again, thus finishing and getting a result. Only after she has stopped racing can she hit a finishing mark with impunity. The crew of the Spanish 470 Olympic gold medal winner threw themselves into the water immediately after finishing. The boat perversely capsized and her mast touched the finishing mark. Fortunately, she was no longer racing, but my heart was in my mouth.

Daisy can only finish 'in the direction of the course from the last *mark*', a rule that regularly gives rise to difficulties. ISAF 102 (Fig 54) shows boat Y sailing a 'hook finish' (that is, her course forms a hook round the mark). Y's course had been prescribed by sailing instructions for a very good reason (to stop classes meeting in opposite directions round the mark), but to no avail. X knew her rules and was the first boat to finish correctly. After claims for redress, the case came to appeal and the RYA, ruling in favour of X, stated: 'It is not open to a race committee to override the definition Finishing.'

This strict principle has to be modified when the race committee lays a line that is virtually in line with the direction from the last mark such that the poor competitor cannot distinguish which is the right way (ISAF 161) (Fig 46).

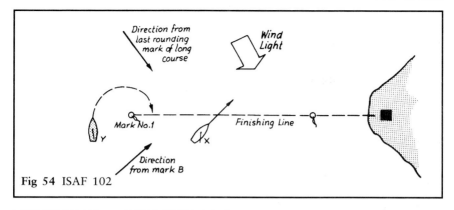

Fig 54 ISAF 102

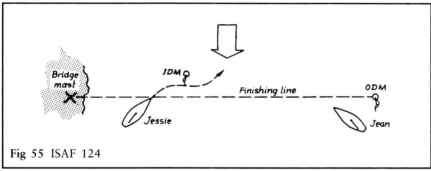

Fig 55 ISAF 124

ISAF 124 (Fig 55) shows us P finishing on a transit line. She finished well beyond the intended position for the limit mark and then passed it on the correct side. The race committee protested her in vain. A mark on the post-finish side of the line did not rank as a mark.

Rule C2.1 alters the definition Finish in match racing.

Interested Party

Given the wide variations in circumstances, this definition is necessarily vague. It deliberately does not specifically state that competitors are interested parties, even though most competitors will stand to gain or lose, however little, from most decisions. It will always be wiser, but not always possible, to choose the protest committee from among those who have not taken part in the race.

Members of the race committee are *not* interested parties; it makes no difference to them who wins or who loses, their interest is with the fleet as a whole. Nevertheless, it is inadvisable to have a member of the race committee serving on the protest committee for a rule 62.1(a) redress hearing, because the race committee itself is a party (in the defined term) to such a hearing and might therefore be considered to be 'interested'.

In RYA 89/10, the appellant believed that the chairman of the protest committee was an interested party because he had warned the appellant on the water that he was breaking the propulsion rule. Dismissing the appeal, this was not accepted: 'The chairman of the protest committee did not stand to gain or lose as a result of the decision. That he witnessed the incident did not debar him from giving evidence, provided he did not do so in the absence of the party.'

As far as 'close personal interest' is concerned, no rule can draw the line between husband and wife at one extreme and cousins three times removed at the other, or know the details of awkward financial dealings between two people. The good judgement of those concerned will decide.

Keep Clear

The give-way boat must keep clear of the right-of-way boat. This definition tells her how to achieve that. She must allow the right-of-way boat to sail without taking avoiding action. If P does not allow S to sail her course without taking avoiding action, she is not keeping clear. Note that this makes no mention of 'proper course'; subject to the constraints of rules 14, 15 and 16, S can sail any course she likes and P must let her. Furthermore, when boats are on the same tack and are very close together, W must not put herself so close to L that L, while able to sail straight ahead, cannot change course without hitting W at once.

ISAF 113 was discussed under rule 10. In ISAF 129, discussed under rule 16, the right-of-way boat altered course suddenly and gave the give-way boat no time to keep clear.

Keeping clear does not mean just avoiding contact; in ISAF 169 (Fig 56), poor S hailed P several times, and when P sailed straight for her, giving no sign of having seen her, S luffed to lessen any damage. At that point, P (one imagines) suddenly realized S was there, bore away frantically, and missed her. S protested under rule 10 and, when that protest was dismissed, appealed. In a long and very interesting decision, the US Appeals Committee upheld the appeal as follows: 'Rule 10 required P to "keep clear" of S. "Keep clear" means something more than "avoid contact"; otherwise the rule would contain those or similar words. Therefore, the fact that the boats did not collide does not necessarily establish that P kept clear. The definition Keep Clear, in combination with the facts, determines whether or not P complied with the rule. In this case, the key question raised by the definition is whether S was able to sail her course "with no need to take avoiding action".

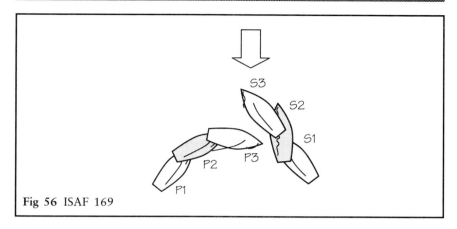

Fig 56 ISAF 169

'The following considerations led to the committee's conclusions and decision:

- the courses of the boats when the incident began. They were on collision courses, which meant that one of them would have to change course.
- the distance between the boats at the moment both boats changed their courses. In the diagram, the distance from P's bow to the leeward side of S, projected forward on the diagram assumption that S would not change course, was approximately two-thirds of P's length.
- the estimated time remaining before contact. When both boats changed course there was very little time remaining before a collision would have occurred. For example, at a speed of five knots (approximately 8.4 feet per second) a 25 foot boat would travel two-thirds of her length in 2.0 seconds. At six knots it would be 1.6 seconds.
- the extent of the course change needed by each boat to avoid a collision. This increased as the boats came closer. At the time P changed course, the change required was such that with her helm "hard over" she passed S's stern "within two feet". At the same moment, the course change S would have needed to avoid P if P did not change course was approximately 90° because S would have had to tack.
- the time required by either boat to make the necessary course change. This factor was itself determined by several others: the boat's weight and speed, her underwater hull shape, the size of her rudder, the sail handling required, and wind and sea conditions.

'In our view, when the boats reached positions P1 and S1 in the diagram, P was not keeping clear. A collision was imminent, and almost unavoidable, as shown by the fact that with helm hard over P passed less than 2 feet from S's stern. At that diagram position, S had no assurance that P had heard her hails, or was preparing to change course, or even that P was aware of the presence of S. Also, P had sailed beyond the point at which she should have borne off, either to minimize the time and distance to reach the windward mark or to sail a course chosen for tactical reasons. For all these reasons, S was clearly unable to sail her course "with no need to take avoiding action". S was fully justified in expecting a collision and in concluding that only her action would prevent it.'

I have no doubt that had P returned S's hail, waved a hand, or tacked, as there was still room to do, S would not have been frightened into luffing and there would have been no incident and no infringement of rule 10. This case puts into proper rule wording a point I have made in protest rooms to P as she was disqualified under rule 10: 'P is not allowed to frighten S.'

Leeward *and* Windward

The leeward side is the side away from the wind, so if you are close-hauled with your boom in its natural position, to port, port is the leeward side of the boat, and if you pull your boom up to starboard, nothing changes and port is still the leeward side and you are still on starboard tack. However, this is not so when sailing downwind or by the lee; leeward then is determined, as it always has been, by the position of the mainsail. The reason is safety. It is essential that *Daisy*, passing a leeward mark and meeting the fleet running down towards

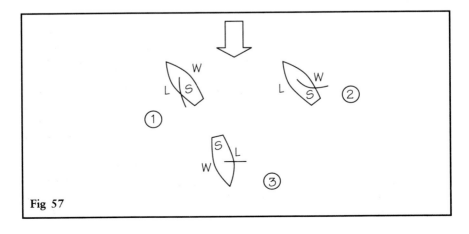

Fig 57

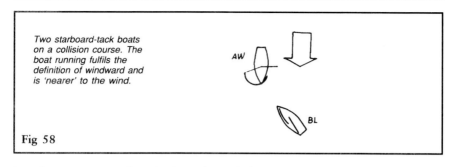

Two starboard-tack boats on a collision course. The boat running fulfils the definition of windward and is 'nearer' to the wind.

AW

BL

Fig 58

her, knows instantly which tack each boat is on. *Daisy* cannot judge whether the boat coming towards her is sailing 'normally' or if she is by the lee, perhaps with her mainsail restrained to stop her gybing. The only question is, since boats like Lasers can sail by the lee at an extraordinary angle to the wind, where does this stop? Fig 57 shows three leeward and windward positions. Position 1, normal; position 2, when the boom is held up against the wind; and position 3, running by the lee. Fig 58 illustrates a very common situation where two boats are sailing towards each other, one having rounded the leeward mark, the other still on the beat. Their closing speed may easily be 15 knots!

Mark

We have looked at marks in some detail in rule 28, but it is a complicated subject, so let us dissect the definition.

1 'An object . . .' The Fastnet Rock, a committee boat and, most commonly, a buoy laid by a race committee, can all be a mark. Even an imaginary point in the North Atlantic can be designated as a turning point to keep boats clear of icebergs.

2 '. . . sailing instructions require a boat to pass . . .' Competitors must know which objects are marks of the course and the information must be expressed clearly and unambiguously in sailing instructions. In RYA 74/1, a two-round course was set: 'ABC – ADC, all marks to port'. When some of the boats went directly from C to A without passing through the starting/finishing line, they were disqualified. Their appeal was upheld; had the race committee wanted the boats to cross the line after rounding C and before reaching A, it should have written 'ABC – ODM – ADC, all marks to port'. Competitors should not be expected to guess what is meant.

3 '. . . on a specified side . . .' It must be clear which side of a mark boats are to go. The ordinary way of doing this is to 'leave the mark to port' (or starboard), meaning of course that the mark will be on the port side of the boat during the passing. 'A port-hand rounding'

151

means the same. This is often abbreviated to: Black Buoy (P), Red Buoy (P). It is not good practice to put, as I saw in sailing instructions the other day, 'passing to starboard of' when you mean 'leave to port'.

4 '. . . objects attached temporarily . . .' In RYA 71/7, a dinghy was lying about seven feet astern of the committee boat. During the race the dinghy was used to move a mark. At the finish, a boat touched it and was disqualified. She appealed successfully: 'The sailing instructions stated that the finishing line would be between the mast and the mark. As they did not specify that the dinghy attached to the committee boat was to be regarded as part of it, the dinghy did not rank as part of the finishing mark.'

The definition covers starting, finishing, limit, passing and boundary marks – and any others if there are any. However, a buoy (or other object) may be specified as a mark in sailing instructions and yet not qualify: a starting limit mark on the pre-start side of the line and a finishing limit mark on the post-finish side of the finishing line may yet not have a required side, and so do not come within the definition.

Obstruction

A piece of paper floating on the water is not an obstruction, but a large rock is. Where is the dividing line? An object that if a boat is sailing directly towards it, and is one hull length away from it, she cannot pass without changing course substantially? This leaves a big area of doubt. Take a tall solid pole some six inches thick; a boat close-hauled can avoid it with the merest twitch of the tiller, while if her spinnaker is set, she might not be able to avoid hitting it. Thus, theoretically, I believe, the same object can be an obstruction, or not, to the same boat. However, I doubt if this matters very much. Sensible sailors and protest committees will always give the benefit of the doubt since this is a question of danger. The danger may be one you can only pass on one side: shoals, sandbanks, jetties etc, or you may be able to go either side of it: a moored boat, or a line of fishing buoys.

Sailing instructions may designate an area that cannot be entered (round the edges of lakes, for instance, where there are bathers and swimmers), and then the line between the boundary marks of this area becomes an invisible obstruction at which a boat may call for water under rule 19.1 just as if she were coming up to a rocky shore.

Other boats can be obstructions too – anything from the *QE2* to an anchored speedboat – but there is a limitation when we come to other boats racing. To be an obstruction, such a boat must be a right-of-way boat or one that is being given room. Look at ISAF 19 (Fig 51); there is P, totally in the wrong, blocking the way for M, and

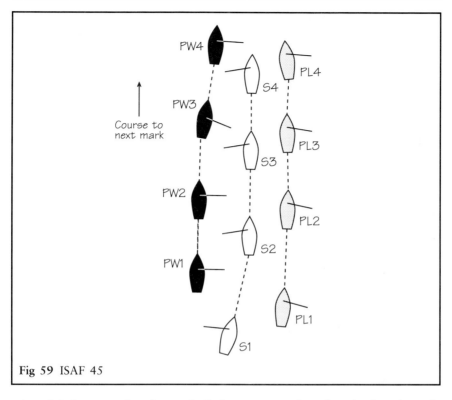

Fig 59 ISAF 45

when M desperately tries to hail for room and tacks, she breaks rule 13 and she cannot use rule 19.1 because P is not a obstruction for her (don't worry, she got off under rule 64.1(b)). In ISAF 45 (Fig 59), S sailed between PL and PW until the boats were running along side by side and then touched. PW protested S under rule 18.5, but rule 10 governed the situation and both PL and PW were disqualified and PW's appeal failed. PW was not an obstruction either to S or PL, because neither of them was required to keep clear of PW. See also ISAF 20, 67 and 91.

Party
Boats that may be penalized (usually the protestee or protestor), boats that have requested redress, and the race committee, when its actions are subject to scrutiny, have certain rights, such as the right to be present at the hearing (rule 63.3), to present evidence (rule 63.6), and to appeal (rule 70). Unless she has requested redress herself (rule 62) or has been offered it by the race or protest committee (rules 60.2

and 60.3), a boat merely dissatisfied with a redress decision is not a party (US 293). Only after she has extracted a decision from the protest committee can she appeal. This is made clear in ISAF 119.

A protestor whose protest is found to be invalid is still a party to the hearing and may appeal the validity of the protest (ISAF 160); while a person who has reported an incident of gross misconduct to the protest committee, under rule 69, is not a party (ISAF 154).

Postpone

A race can be postponed at any time until the starting signal; a postponement may last five minutes or a day or more – though usually if it lasts for more it will be formally abandoned. Its use is controlled by rule 27.3 (and Appendix E). It is signalled by AP. AP over H signals that the races that have already started can be finished and everyone else should go home. AP over A again is addressed only to races not started, meaning that there will be no more racing that day. AP over a numeral pennant tells you how long the postponement will be. The time runs from the scheduled starting time. Thus if a race scheduled for 1030 is postponed for one hour and then for another, the second hoist will be AP over 2, meaning 1230 for the start.

If the race officer makes a mistake in the starting procedure, he is allowed to signal a general recall (rule 29.3), but when the Z or black flag penalties are in force (rule 30), a postponement, even one second before the gun is preferable. It will save competitors from being unnecessarily penalised.

Proper Course

It is very common for two boats in the same class, sailing the same race, to have different proper courses. Those who race in tidal waters will be well aware of this. (Is the north shore better than the south shore, who knows?) ISAF 25 (Fig 15) shows L and W, each on a proper course. 'Which of the two courses is the faster one to the finish,' said the RYA, 'cannot be determined in advance, and is not necessarily proven by one boat or the other reaching the next mark ahead.' (Under rule 11 we see that when each boat is on a proper course and these courses converge, it is W that must keep clear.)

Again, US 74 discusses the obligations of two boats when not on a beat to windward, stating: 'The proper course below which W was not permitted to sail (rule 17.2) and above which L was not permitted to sail (rule 17.1), while having the same objective, was not necessarily the same proper course. The mark was a considerable distance away and they were carrying different sails. Both facts could have a bearing on what each construed to be her proper course.'

US 79 (Fig 18) shows how a current can make a course 'proper', even though the boat does not point towards the mark; and RYA 69/9 similarly states: 'The definition Proper Course refers to the course made good through the water, not in the direction in which she is pointing.'

Normally, this proper course will not be above close-hauled, but at the mark this may not be so. RYA 75/6 (Fig 60) shows L luffing head to wind, sails empty, in order to try to shoot the mark. In doing so, she hit W. W maintained that L took room to which she was not entitled, and the race committee asked whether L was sailing a proper course and whether the phrase 'to *finish* as soon as possible' included pinching, shooting head to wind, or generally wriggling round the mark during the existence of an overlap. The RYA, to put it briefly, replied, 'Yes; since even without the presence of W, L would have sailed similarly.'

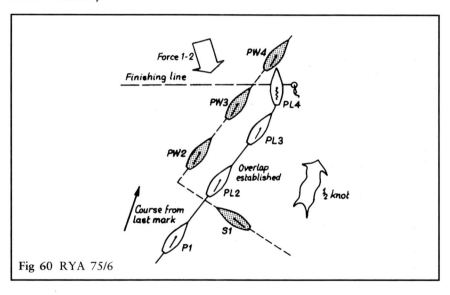

Fig 60 RYA 75/6

Any course that a boat sails merely because of the other boat in the rule (for example, W in rule 17.1 or L in rule 17.2) is not a proper course. But if *Daisy* has to sail wide at a mark to avoid a bunch of boats ahead of her, that will be a proper course.

Protest

The term covers any action brought by a boat, a race committee or a protest committee against a boat they believe has broken a rule. It does not include actions under rule 69 or requests for redress. (Note that it does not mention a boat protesting the race committee, because such a thing is not possible.)

Racing

Phrases such as 'while racing', 'when racing' and 'not racing' used in various rules necessitate identifying the precise moment at which racing begins or ends.

Racing begins at the same instant for all boats: at the preparatory signal. Boats milling around near the starting line are, for obvious reasons of safety, already subject to the rules of Part 2 (see preamble to Part 2) rather than to IRPCS, but only at the preparatory signal do they become liable to penalization for breaking a rule.

Racing can end at the same time for everyone, when a race is postponed, abandoned or a general recall is signalled; but when all is well, it ends at an individual time for each boat: when she has finished or retired. She must clear the line (in either direction – rule 28.1) and the marks before she can safely consider herself as no longer racing.

US 99 (Fig 48) looked at the phrase '. . . and clears the finishing line . . .' P luffed head to wind to finish, her genoa came aback and she was forced on to port tack. S, straddling the line, hit her, and protested under rule 13. It was clear that P had infringed either rule 13 or rule 10, but was she still racing and therefore subject to disqualification? The US Appeals Committee stated, 'When no part of a boat's hull, equipment or crew is still on the finishing line she has cleared it', and it was held that she was not racing. Neither boat was close to a finishing mark.

US 136 (Fig 49) discusses the phrase 'clears . . . the finishing marks'. A boat was disqualified for touching a finishing mark and not exonerating herself. 'The intent of including finishing marks,' said the US Appeals Committee, 'as one of the criteria in determining when a boat is no longer racing is to prevent a boat which finishes so close to a mark that she is unable to avoid touching it, from escaping penalty by having cleared the line at the time of touching. In this case the boat was some six lengths from the mark she subsequently touched. When she cleared the line she was well clear of the mark. Thus her contact with the mark was no part of her finishing manoeuvre. It was a separate incident, occurring when she was no longer racing.'

If you are wondering if a boat is racing or not, ask yourself whether, if she had an engine, you would be happy for her to start motoring.

Room

This is a simple definition, discussed further under rule 18.2(a); comment is perhaps worthwhile on two points:

1 '... in the existing conditions ...' The inside dinghy rounding a mark on a calm day with no sea will need little more than her own beam width; but in open water with steep seas and a strong wind, approaching a mark that is being tossed about wildly and unpredictably, the inside boat will need at least a boat length, if not more, to ensure safety.

2 '... promptly in a seamanlike way ...' The boat giving the room must provide enough space so that the other need not make extraordinary or abnormal manoeuvres to keep clear of her or, when appropriate, of the mark. But the boat taking room is not allowed space either to manoeuvre slowly, perhaps doing nothing about getting her spinnaker down until she is past the mark, or incompetently, perhaps getting a spinnaker wrap, or dropping the genoa overboard, neither of which could be considered seamanlike. This is discussed more fully in ISAF 40.

Rule

(a) Any statement in the whole of the rules book is a rule except 'Sportsmanship and the Rules', which lays down a principle, and the titles to the rules. These are informative, and should not be taken into account when interpreting a rule. Appendices N and P are also consultative.

(b) National authority prescriptions are mainly addressed to organizing authorities and race committees; few relate to competitors. At an international event, competitors are entitled to a copy of the prescriptions in English.

(c) Sailing instructions have already been discussed under rule 88.2.

(d) Classes often have two sets of rules: measurement and championship. The latter will cover such matters as crews, special safety regulations, number and types of courses to be sailed, etc. Class rules may alter or add to RRS only when specifically allowed by rule 86.3.

(e) Other documents may – and pity the poor sailor – include the notice of race, safety regulations, local authority by-laws, club by-laws – and goodness knows what else.

In RYA 89/6, some boats anchored in an area marked on the chart as prohibited; they were protested and disqualified. On appeal, they were reinstated; the 'other documents' mentioned in paragraph (e) of the definition had to be specifically prescribed in the sailing instructions before they could become mandatory for racing. Local authorities were free to prosecute the boats under the by-laws if they saw fit. It is important to provide competitors with adequate information on these matters and, where pre-race preparation is necessary, only fair to give advance warning in the notice of race.

Start

1 'A boat *starts* . . .' *Daisy* cannot start unless she starts in accordance with this definition. She can begin, commence, but not *start*!

2 '. . . after her starting signal . . .' If *Daisy* crosses the line before the signal, she has not started; she will be scored 'on the course side' (OCS) and must either return and start unless one of the penalty systems is in force when she will have other penalties.

3 '. . . any part of her hull, crew or equipment . . .' This includes *Daisy*'s anchor if she is kedged with the anchor on the course side of the line. Note that the words 'in normal position', found in 'Clear Astern and Clear Ahead' and 'Finish', are missing. In a downwind start, an escaped spinnaker blowing out in front will put her over the line.

4 '. . . she has complied with rule 29.1 and rule 30.1 if it applies.' Rule 29.1 explains what she must do if she is over the line on a normal start; 30.1 requires her to go 'round the ends'.

Tack, Starboard *or* Port

Daisy must be either on port or on starboard tack. There is no other situation. When starboard is her windward side, she is on starboard tack; when port is her windward side, she is on port tack. But be careful, and check 'Leeward and Windward' for an anomaly when boats are running by the lee.

When *Daisy* luffs head to wind and stays there, she remains on the tack she has been on until she passes through head to wind as is made clear by rule 13. In US 138 (Fig 61), A was head to wind by the mark when B arrived and nudged her round into tacking. Since A was still head to wind when she was hit, she was not yet subject to rule 13 and was still on port tack. B was disqualified under rule 18.2(b) for failing to keep clear.

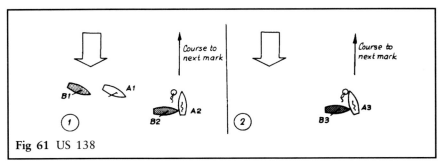

Fig 61 US 138

Two-Length Zone

A convenient short cut, it is cut even shorter in this book, where the two-length zone is usually just called 'the circle'.

Rule E4 alters the definition to *four-length zone* for radio-controlled boat racing.

Appendices

The appendices are many and long; readers will find them in *The Racing Rules of Sailing* in the ISAF edition, or in the rules of their own national authority. The appendices are mostly specialized and many of them consist of information that is not needed in a hurry and therefore can be studied at leisure. Only Appendix A, F and G are printed in full.

Appendix A – Scoring

See rule 88.3.

A1 GENERAL SCORING RULES
These rules apply regardless of the scoring system in effect.

A1.1 Failure to Start or Finish
When the race committee scores a boat as failing to *start* or *finish* it need not protest her.

A1.2 Boat Retiring or Disqualified After Finishing
When a boat retires or is disqualified after *finishing*, each boat that *finished* after her shall be moved up one place.

A1.3 Scores Not Discardable
When a scoring system provides that one or more race scores are to be discarded in calculating a boat's series score, the score for disqualification under rule 2, or rule 42 when rule 67 applies, shall not be discarded.

A1.4 Unbroken Ties

(a) When boats are tied at the end of a race, the points for the place for which the boats have tied and for the place(s) immediately below shall be added together and divided equally. Boats tied for a prize shall share it or receive equal prizes.

(b) When boats have equal scores at the end of a series and a tie is unbroken by the scoring system, the scores shall remain unchanged in the final results. Boats tied for a prize shall share it or receive equal prizes.

A1.5 Numbering of Races

Races shall be numbered sequentially in the order of completion.

A1.6 A Boat's Starting Time

The time of a boat's starting signal shall be used as her starting time.

A1.7 Scores Removed from All or Part of a Series

When a boat is penalized by having her scores removed from the results of some or all races of a series, no changes shall be made in the race scores of other boats.

A2 SCORING SYSTEMS

The Bonus Point Scoring System and the Low Point Scoring System are the systems most often used. The bonus point system gives extra points for the first six places because it is harder to sail from fourth place into third, for example, than from fourteenth place into thirteenth. It is used for many class championships. The low point system is also suitable for championships, is better for small-fleet racing and is easier to use. Both systems are primarily designed for regattas but may be adapted for other series; see rule A5.

Either system may be made applicable by stating in the sailing instructions that the bonus point or low point system of Appendix A of the racing rules will apply and including the information required in rule A2.1.

A2.1 Number of Races and Series Scores

The number of races scheduled and the number required to constitute a series shall be stated in the sailing instructions. Each boat's series score will be the total of her race scores, discarding her worst score* except when prohibited in rule A1.3. The lowest series score wins.

* More than one score may be required to be discarded or all scores may be required to be counted; in either case the sailing instructions shall so state.

A2.2 Race Scores

Each boat *starting* and *finishing* in a race, and not thereafter retiring or being disqualified, will be scored points as follows:

Finishing place system	*Bonus point system*	*Low point*
First	0	1
Second	3	2
Third	5.7	3
Fourth	8	4
Fifth	10	5
Sixth	11.7	6
Seventh	13	7
Each place thereafter	Add 1 point	Add 1 point

All other boats will be scored points for the finishing place one more than the total number of boats entered in the series.

A2.3 Ties

When there is a tie in series points between two or more boats, the tie will be broken in favour of the boat with the most first places, or, if the tie remains, the most second places, or lower places if necessary, using only the scores for each boat that count for her series score. When a tie still remains, it will be broken in favour of the boat with the best score in the last race in which the tied boats *raced* and scored differently, using only the scores for each boat that count for her series score. For these calculations, if a boat has been awarded average points that do not correspond to a place, she shall be considered to have the place closest in points to the points awarded; if a boat has tied for a place, she shall be considered to have that place.

A3 ABBREVIATIONS FOR SCORING RECORDS

These abbreviations are recommended for recording the circumstances that determine a score:

DNC Did not come to the starting area
DNS Did not *start*
OCS On the course side of the starting line and failed to comply with rule 29.1 or rule 30.1
DNF Did not *finish*
RET Retired after *finishing*
DSQ Disqualified
DND Disqualification not discardable because of rule A1.3
RDG Redress given
ZPG Z flag penalty given

A4 REDRESS

If under rule 64.2 the protest committee decides to change a boat's score, it should consider scoring her

(a) points equal to the average, to the nearest tenth of a point (0.05 to be rounded upward), of her points in all the races in the series except [her worst race and]* the race in question, or

(b) points equal to the average, to the nearest tenth of a point (0.05 to be rounded upward), of her points in all the races before the race in question, or

(c) points based on the position of the boat at the time of the incident that justified the redress.

*   Delete these words when all scores count for series results, or adjust when more than one race is to be discarded.

A5 WHEN A SERIES IS NOT A REGATTA

In a regatta all boats are expected to compete in all races and the difference between the number of entrants and the number of starters is usually insignificant. However, in a longer series there may be a number of boats that compete in fewer races than others, in which case the following may be substituted for the second paragraph of rule A2.2:

> Boats not so scored that came to the starting area will be scored points for the finishing place one more than the number of all boats that came to the starting area. Boats that did not come to the starting area will be scored points for the finishing place one more than the number of boats entered in the series.

Appendix A can be changed by national authority prescriptions or by sailing instructions. Rule A1 contains rules that everyone needs to know. They do not need explaining, but should be read with care to avoid any unpleasant surprises at the end of a race. There is no default scoring system, so either one of the two systems given, or one of the many others in use, must be prescribed in sailing instructions. The new abbreviations will probably come to be used worldwide.

Appendix B – Sailboard Racing Rules

Appendix C – Match Racing Rules

Appendix D – Team Racing Rules

Appendix E – Radio-Controlled Boat Racing Rules
These four appendices are for specialized kinds of racing, each of which needs its own rules. These rules can all be changed by national authority prescription or by sailing instructions, except those that change a rule already made immutable by rule 86.1.

Appendix F – Appeals Procedure
The appendix may be changed by national authority prescription, but not by sailing instructions.

See rule 70. A national authority may change this appendix by prescription but it shall not be changed by sailing instructions.

F1   NATIONAL AUTHORITY
Appeals, requests by protest committees for confirmation or correction of decisions, and requests for the interpretation of *rules* shall be made to the national authority.

F2 APPELLANT'S RESPONSIBILITIES

F2.1 Within 15 days of receiving the protest committee's written decision or its decision not to reopen a hearing, the appellant shall send a dated appeal to the national authority with a copy of the protest committee's decision. The appeal shall state why the appellant believes the protest committee's interpretation of a *rule* or its procedures were incorrect.

F2.2 The appellant shall also send, with the appeal or as soon as possible thereafter, any of the following documents that are available to her:

(a) the written *protest(s)*;

(b) a diagram, prepared or endorsed by the protest committee, showing the positions and tracks of all boats involved, the course to the next *mark* and its required side, the force and direction of the wind, and, if relevant, the depth of water and direction and speed of any current;

(c) the notice of race, the sailing instructions, any other conditions governing the event, and any changes to them;

(d) any additional relevant documents; and

(e) the names and addresses of all *parties* to the hearing and the protest committee chairman.

F2.3 A request from a protest committee for confirmation or correction of its decision shall include the decision and all relevant documents. A request for a *rule* interpretation shall include assumed facts.

F3 NOTIFICATION AND RESPONSE OF THE PROTEST COMMITTEE
Upon receipt of an appeal, the national authority shall send a copy of the appeal to the protest committee, asking the protest committee for the documents listed in rule F2.2 not supplied by the appellant, and the protest committee shall send the documents to the national authority.

F4 NATIONAL AUTHORITY'S RESPONSIBILITIES
The national authority shall send copies of the appeal and the protest committee's decision to the other *parties* to the hearing. It shall send to the appellant copies of documents not sent by the appellant. It shall send to any *party* to the hearing upon request any of the documents listed in rule F2.2.

F5 ADDITIONAL INFORMATION
The national authority shall accept the protest committee's finding of facts except when it decides they are inadequate, in which case it may require the protest committee to provide additional facts or other information, or to reopen the hearing and report any new finding of facts.

F6   COMMENTS
Parties to the hearing and the protest committee may send comments on the appeal to the national authority, provided they do so within 15 days of receiving the appeal. The national authority shall send such comments to all *parties* to the hearing and to the protest committee.

F7   WITHDRAWING AN APPEAL
An appellant may withdraw an appeal before it is decided by accepting the protest committee's decision.

Appendix G – Advertising
The appendix may not be changed, but may be overridden by governmental requirements.

See Rule 79. This appendix shall not be changed by sailing instructions or prescriptions of national authorities. When governmental requirements conflict with parts of it, those requirements apply.

G1   DEFINITION OF ADVERTISING
For the purposes of this appendix, advertising is the name, logo, slogan, description, depiction, a variation or distortion thereof, or any other form of communication that promotes an organization, person, product, service, brand or idea so as to call attention to it or to persuade persons or organizations to buy, approve or otherwise support it.

G2   GENERAL
G2.1 Advertisements and anything advertised shall meet generally accepted moral and ethical standards.

G2.2 This appendix shall apply when *racing* and, in addition, unless otherwise stated in the notice of race, from 0700 on the first race day of a regatta until the expiry of the time limit for lodging *protests* following the last race of the regatta.

G2.3 An event shall be designated Category A, B or C in its notice of race and sailing instructions, but if not so designated it shall be Category A. However, at the world and continental championships of Olympic classes, Category B advertising shall be permitted on hulls and, for Olympic sailboard classes, on hulls and sails. After the notice of race has been published, the category shall not be changed within ninety days before the event without prior approval of the national authority of the organizing authority.

G2.4   A national authority, or a class of the Offshore Racing Council for its events, may prescribe *rules* for advertising that are more restrictive than those of a category. For a particular event, the notice of race and the sailing instructions may include *rules* for advertising that are more restrictive that those of the event's category.

G2.5   Advertisements on sails shall be clearly separated from national letters and sail numbers.

G2.6   When, after finding the facts, a protest committee decides that a boat or her crew has broken a rule of this appendix, it shall

(a)   warn the boat that another breach of the rule will result in disqualification; or

(b)   disqualify the boat in accordance with rule 64.1; or

(c)   disqualify the boat from more than one race or from the series when it decides that the breach warrants a stronger penalty; or

(d)   act under rule 69.1 when it decides that there may have been a gross breach.

G2.7   The ISAF, a national authority, a class association or the ORC may, for its events, subject to rule G5, designate the category and may require a fee for doing so.

G2.8   The ISAF or a national authority may, for its events, prescribe *rules* and require a fee for giving consent to individual boats for advertisements, provided that such consents do not conflict with, when relevant, class rules or the rules of the ORC.

G3   **CATEGORY A**
G3.1   Advertising on boats other than sailboards is permitted only as follows:

(a)   The boat's class insignia may be displayed on her sails as required by Appendix H.

(b)   One sailmaker's mark, which may include the name or mark of the sailcloth manufacturer and the pattern or model of the sail, may be displayed on both sides of any sail and shall fit within a 150mm × 150mm square. On sails other than spinnakers, no part of such mark shall be placed farther from the tack than the greater of 300mm or 15% of the length of the foot.

(c)   One builder's mark, which may include the name or mark of the designer, may be placed on the hull, and one maker's mark may be displayed on spars and on each side of small equipment. Such marks shall fit within a 150mm × 150mm square.

(d) The boat's type may be displayed on each side of her hull. Lettering shall not be higher than 1% or longer than 5% of the hull length of the boat, to a maximum of 100mm or 70mm respectively.

(e) Makers' marks may be displayed on clothing and equipment. Other advertising may be displayed on clothing and equipment ashore.

(f) The organizing authority of a sponsored event may permit or require the display of an advertisement of the event sponsor not larger than $0.27m^2$ in the form of a flag, and/or of a decal or sticker attached to each side of the hull or to a dodger on each side of the boat. In addition, when a sponsor supplies all hulls and sails at no cost to the organizing authority or competitors, one advertisement not larger than $0.27m^2$ may be displayed on each side of the mainsail. For an event of a class association or the ORC and, when it so prescribes, by the national authority concerned. Notice of such permission or requirement shall be included in the notice of race and the sailing instructions.

G3.2 Advertising on sailboards is permitted only as follows:

(a) The sailboard's class insignia may be displayed on her sail as required in Appendix H.

(b) One sailmaker's mark, which may include the name or mark of the sailcloth manufacturer and the pattern or model of the sail, may be displayed on both sides of the sail. No part of such a mark shall be placed farther from the tack than 20% of the length of the foot of the sail, including the mast sleeve. The mark may also be displayed on the lower half of the part of the sail above the wishbone but no part of it shall be farther than 500mm from the clew.

(c) The sailboard's type or manufacturer's name or logo may be placed on the hull in two places and on the upper third of the part of the sail above the wishbone. One maker's mark may be displayed on the spars, on each side of small equipment and on a competitor's clothing and harness.

(d) The organizing authority of a sponsored event may permit or require the display of an advertisement of the event sponsor on both sides of the sail between the sail numbers and the wishbone and on a bib worn by the competitor. For an event of a class association, such advertising requires approval by the class association and, when it so prescribes, by the national authority concerned. Notice of such permission or requirement shall be included in the notice of race and the sailing instructions.

G4   CATEGORY B

G4.1 A boat competing in a Category B event may display advertising only as permitted for Category A and by rule G4.2 (for boats other than sailboards) or rule G4.3 (for sailboards) and throughout that event shall not display advertising chosen by the boat of more than two organizations or persons. A Category B advertisement shall be either one or two of

(a) the name of an organization or person,

(b) a brand or product name, or

(c) a logo.

G4.2 Advertising on Boats Other Than Sailboards

(a) The forward 25% of each side of the hull may display no more than two advertisements chosen by the ISAF, the national authority, the class association or the ORC, for its event; or by the organizing authority of the event when it wishes to display advertising of an event sponsor. When both the organizing authority and one of the other organizations wish to use the space, they shall each be entitled to half the length of the space on each side. The remaining length of the hull shall be free of any advertising except for that permitted in rule G3.1(c) and except that half that length may be used for advertising chosen by the boat. If advertising is not displayed on the sides of the hull, it may be displayed on each side of the cabin, the insides of the cockpit coamings or sidetanks, subject to the same length dimensions.

(b) Advertising chosen by the boat may be displayed on sails as follows:

(1) Advertising on spinnakers is without restriction except as provided in rules G2.5 and G4.

(2) On one other sail, only one advertisement may be carried at a time, and it may be on both sides of the sail. It shall be placed below the national letters and sail numbers and have a width no greater than two-thirds of the length of the foot of the sail and a height no greater than one-third of that width.

(c) Advertising chosen by the boat may be displayed on the mainmast and main boom, but both displays shall be limited to the name, brand or product name, or logo of one organization. The space within one-third of the length of the mast and two-thirds of the length of the boom may be used.

(d) In addition to the advertisements carried on the boat, advertisements limited to the organization(s) advertising on the boat and one or two additional organizations may be displayed on clothing and equipment worn by competitors.

G4.3   Advertising on Sailboards

(a)   The forward 25% of the hull may display no more than two advertisements chosen by the ISAF, the national authority or the class association for its event; or by the organizing authority of the event when it wishes to display advertising of an event sponsor. When both the organizing authority and one of the other organizations wish to use the space, they shall each be entitled to half the length of the space on each side. Advertising chosen by the competitor may be displayed within the remaining length of the hull.

(b)   That part of the sail below the wishbone not used for Category A advertising may display advertising chosen by the competitor.

(c)   In addition to the advertisements carried on the sailboard, advertisements limited to the organization(s) advertising on the sailboard and one or two additional organizations may be displayed on clothing and equipment worn by competitors.

G5   CATEGORY C ADVERTISING

G5.1   Approval of Advertising

Advertising for a Category C event (any event that permits advertising beyond Category B advertising) shall be

(a)   approved by the national authority of the venue unless the event is an international event;

(b)   approved by the International Sailing Federation (ISAF) when the event is an international event (i.e., an event open to entries other than those from the national authority of the venue).

G5.2   Advertising Fees

(a)   National events: The national authority of the venue may require an advertising fee for approval of Category C advertising to be paid to it.

(b)   International events: The ISAF will require an advertising fee for approval of Category C advertising, and will share the fee equally with the national authority of the venue.

G5.3   Approval Fees

The organizing authority of an event with cash or cashable prizes or appearance payments totalling more than US$10,000 or the equivalent may be required to pay an approval fee. For a national event the national authority of the venue may require such a fee to be paid to it. For an international event the ISAF will require such a fee to be paid to it.

G5.4 Rules for Category C advertising shall be stated in the notice of race and the sailing instructions.

Appendix H – Identification on Sails
The appendix may be changed by sailing instructions or national authority prescriptions, but not by class rules except as provided in the appendix itself. It concerns the letters and numbers on sails.

Appendix J – Weighing Clothing and Equipment
This appendix is addressed to measurers checking on the requirements of rule 43.1(b). It cannot be changed.

Appendix K – Competitors' ISAF Eligibility
The appendix cannot be changed. It refers to professional sailors and to those found guilty under rule 5 (drugs) or rule 69.2 (gross misconduct).

Appendix L – Banned Substances and Banned Methods
This doping appendix cannot be changed, but may be overridden by governmental requirements.

Appendix M – Notice of Race and Sailing Instructions
This appendix is a long list of things that must be included in the two documents. It can be altered, but it is probably never necessary to do so. It is addressed to the organizing authority and the race committee.

Appendix N – Sailing Instructions Guide
This guide provides a tested set of sailing instructions designed primarily for major championship regattas for one or more classes.
  The principles on which it rests are in the comment to rule 88.2.

Appendix P – Recommendations for Protest Committees
This appendix is advisory only and is addressed to protest committee chairmen, and in particular those who have not much experience of protest work.

Appendix Q – International Juries
This appendix cannot be changed. It lays down the requirements for setting up and running an international jury.

Index

This is an index of the words and phrases used in the racing rules. It refers to the rule number, not the page number, and can, therefore, be used with this or any other book in which the rules are printed. Do not try to use this index instead of the rules; it should guide you to the rule you want, but does not pretend to tell you what the rule says.

References are given in the order they appear in the book and are to rules (eg 27.3), Appendices (eg A1.4 or B) or sections (eg Introduction). Page numbers for sections can be found in the Contents. Italics are used for words that appear in the Definitions. Appendices B, C, D, E, J, M, N and P are not indexed in detail.